Klaus Hinrichsen

NAVY NCIS

NCIS TV-Show Fan Book DVD Season 1 - 8

★ ★ ★

December 2011
Klaus Hinrichsen

The book is based on articles from magazines, newspapers and other books as well as the Internet. Although the author never intended to use any lines from the various sources without stating so, it cannot be totally ruled out, that the one or other great line, read in the odd article, found its way into the book by pure chance. With this book the author only tried to give all the NCIS fans a complete book on the NCIS-TV-series seasons1-8. The author holds no connection what so ever with Belisarius Productions, CBS Broadcasting or Paramount Pictures.

Hinrichsen, Klaus

NAVY NCIS

NCIS TV-Show Fan Book DVD Season 1 - 8

December 2011
Klaus Hinrichsen

***

Herstellung und Verlag: Books on Demand GmbH, Norderstedt
Produced and published by Books on Demand GmbH, Norderstedt, Germany
Printed in Germany

ISBN: 978-3-8448-0430-0

Content

Content

Premise

NCIS, formerly known as NCIS: Naval Criminal Investigative Service, is an American police procedural drama television series revolving around a fictional team of special agents from the Naval Criminal Investigative Service, which conducts criminal investigations involving the U.S. Navy and Marine Corps. The concept and characters were initially introduced in a two-part episode of the CBS series JAG (JAG episodes 8.20 and 8.21). The show, a spin-off from JAG, premiered on September 23, 2003 on CBS and, to date, has aired eight full seasons and has gone into syndicated reruns on USA Network, Cloo (formerly Sleuth) and Ion Television. Donald Bellisario, who created JAG as well as the well-known series Airwolf, Magnum, P.I. and Quantum Leap, is co-creator and executive producer of NCIS. NCIS was originally referred to as Navy NCIS during Season 1; however, "Navy" was later dropped from the title as it was redundant. NCIS was joined in its seventh season by a spin-off series, NCIS: Los Angeles, starring Chris O'Donnell and LL Cool J.

NCIS follows a fictional team of Naval Criminal Investigative Service Major Case Response Team (MCRT) special agents headquartered at the Washington Navy Yard in Washington, D.C. It is described by the actors and producers (on special features on DVD releases in the United States) as being distinguished by its comic elements, ensemble acting and character-driven plots.
NCIS is the primary law enforcement and counter-intelligence arm of the United States Department of the Navy, which includes the United States Marine Corps. NCIS investigates all major criminal offenses (felonies)—crimes punishable under the Uniform Code of Military Justice by confinement of more than one year—within the Department of the Navy. The MCRT is frequently assigned to high profile cases such as the death of the U.S. president's military aide, a bomb situation on a U.S. Navy warship, the death of a celebrity on a reality show set on a USMC base, terrorist threats, and kidnappings.
The MCRT is led by Supervisory Special Agent Leroy Jethro Gibbs (Mark Harmon). Gibbs's team is composed of Special Agent and Senior Field Agent Anthony "Tony" DiNozzo (Michael Weatherly), Special Agent Timothy McGee (Sean Murray) and Special Agent (formerly Mossad liaison officer) Ziva David (Cote de Pablo), who replaced Caitlin "Kate" Todd (Sasha Alexander) when she was shot and killed by rogue Mossad agent Ari Haswari (Rudolf Martin) at the end of season two. The team is assisted in their investigations by Chief Medical Examiner Donald "Ducky" Mallard (David McCallum), his assistant Jimmy Palmer (Brian Dietzen), who replaced Gerald Jackson (Pancho Demmings), and Forensic Specialist Abigail "Abby" Sciuto (Pauley Perrette).

It has been revealed through flashbacks that the 'original' head of the MCRT was Special Agent Mike Franks (Muse Watson), who led the unit when it was part of the Naval Investigative Service (NIS), the predecessor agency of the NCIS. He recruited Gibbs shortly after Gibbs' retirement from the Marine Corps, eventually retiring himself some years later. After Franks' departure, Gibbs recruited DiNozzo from the Baltimore Police Department's Homicide Section. The two were briefly joined by Vivian Blackadder (Robyn Lively), whom Gibbs recruited from the FBI. In the second part of the NCIS pilot, Blackadder allowed her emotions to nearly derail an anti-terror operation in Spain. Gibbs is noticeably disappointed; Blackadder is not present in the series' first regular episode, replaced by Caitlin Todd, a Secret Service agent who joins Gibbs' team after resigning from the Secret Service. McGee first appears as a Field Agent assigned to the Norfolk Field Office. He uses his computer skills to aid the MCRT in subsequent investigations through the rest of the first season, until he is officially promoted with his own desk at the Navy Yard in the beginning of the second season.

NCIS is currently led by Director Leon Vance (Rocky Carroll). The first director seen in the series, Thomas Morrow (Alan Dale), left after being promoted to Deputy Director of the Department of Homeland Security. Jenny Shepard (Lauren Holly) was appointed director after Morrow in the first episode of season three. After Shepard was killed in a shootout at the end of the fifth season Vance, who was Assistant Director of NCIS before her death, was seen as Acting Director after her death and was promoted to take her place.

Source: [1]

Main Cast

Name	Portrayed by	Episodes Main	Seasons Main	Episodes Recurring	Seasons Recurring
Special Agent Leroy Jethro **Gibbs**	Mark Harmon	001–	1–		
Special Agent Anthony „**Tony**" DiNozzo	Michael Weatherly	001–	1–		
Abigail „**Abby**" Sciuto	Pauley Perrette	001–	1–		
Dr. Donald „**Ducky**" Mallard	David McCallum	001–	1–		
Special Agent Caitlin „**Kate**" Todd	Sasha Alexander	001–46	1–2	047–48	3
Special Agent Timothy „Tim" **McGee**	Sean Murray	024	2	007, 11, 18–23	1
Special Agent **Ziva** David	Cote de Pablo	050–	3–	047–48	3
Director Jennifer „**Jenny**" Shepard	Lauren Holly	055–113	3–5	047–54	3
Director Leon **Vance**	Rocky Carroll	114–	6–	108–109, 111, 113	5
Jimmy **Palmer**	Brian Dietzen [a]	114–	6–	021–113	1–5

[a] also starring

Source: [1]

Recurring Cast

From Season 1:

- Joe Spano as Tobias Fornell (1–)
- Alan Dale as Thomas Morrow (1–3)
- Rudolf Martin as Ari Haswari (1–3)
- Jessica Steen as Paula Cassidy (1–4)
- Pancho Demmings as Gerald Jackson (1, 3)

From Season 2:

- Troian Bellisario as Sarah McGee (2, 4)
- Tamara Taylor as Cassie Yates (2–3)

From Season 3:

- Michael Bellisario as Charles „Chip" Sterling (3)
- Muse Watson as Mike Franks (3–)
- Don Franklin as Ron Sacks (3–4)

From Season 4:

- Liza Lapira as Michelle Lee (4–6)
- Scottie Thompson as Jeanne Benoit (4–5)
- Susanna Thompson as Hollis Mann (4–5)
- David Dayan Fisher as Trent Kort (4–)
- Armand Assante as René Benoit (4–5)

From Season 5:

- Susan Kelechi Watson as Nicki Jardine (5)
- Paul Telfer as Damon Werth (5, 7)
- Jonathan LaPaglia as Brent Langer (5–6)

From Season 6:

- Merik Tadros as Michael Rivkin (6)
- Michael Nouri as Eli David (6–)
- Ralph Waite as Jackson Gibbs (6–)
- Jude Ciccolella as SecNav Phillip Davenport (6, 8)

From Season 7:

- Robert Wagner as Anthony D. DiNozzo Sr. (7–)
- Rena Sofer as M. Allison Hart (7)
- Dina Meyer as Holly Snow (7)
- Marco Sanchez as Alejandro Rivera (7–8)
- Diane Neal as Abigail Borin (7–)
- T.J. Ramini as Malachi Ben-Gidon (7–)
- Jacqueline Obradors as Paloma Reynosa (7–8)

From Season 8:

- David Sullivan as Larry Krone (8)
- Annie Wersching as Gail Walsh (8)
- Sarah Jane Morris as Erica Jane „E.J." Barrett (8–)
- Enrique Murciano as Ray Cruz (8–)
- Wendy Makkena as Dr. Rachel Cranston (8–)
- Matthew Willig as Simon Cade (8–9)
- Matt Craven as SecNav Clayton Jarvis (8–)

Source: [1]

Name: Leroy Jethro Gibbs

Occupation:	Supervisory/Senior Special Agent in Charge (NCIS), Former Gunnery Sergeant (Marine sniper and Military Police)(USMC)
Gender:	Male
Family:	Jackson Gibbs (Father)
Spouse(s):	Shannon Gibbs (deceased) Diane Sterling (divorced) Unknown (divorced) Stephanie Flynn (divorced)
Children:	Kelly Gibbs (deceased)

Supervisory Special Agent Leroy Jethro Gibbs, portrayed by Mark Harmon, was born in Stillwater, Pennsylvania to Jackson Gibbs and an unnamed mother. He joined the United States Marine Corps in 1976 and became a Scout Sniper instead of attending college. After serving tours of duty in Panama and Iraq, he retired from the Marine Corps with the rank of Gunnery Sergeant. He joined NIS, which later became NCIS, after his wife Shannon and only daughter Kelly were murdered in 1991. Gibbs later travelled to Mexico and murdered the drug dealer responsible, a crime he kept concealed for twenty years. Since then, he has been married and divorced three times, and is currently single.
He currently leads a team consisting of Anthony DiNozzo, Timothy McGee, Abigail Sciuto, and Ziva David. In the episode "Bête Noire" Gibbs comes face to face with terrorist Ari Haswari and puts a bullet through Ari's left shoulder. Finding Ari later becomes an obsession for Gibbs when he and DiNozzo witness original team member Agent Kate Todd get shot dead in front of them in the season 2 finale, "Twilight".
He is often shown in his basement building boats, at least one of which he named after his daughter; another was named after one of his ex-wives. In the episode "Blowback", when confronting "Goliath" on the plane about "ARES", Gibbs revealed he is a Virgo. He is a deadshot marksman, as evidenced in "Hiatus" with flashbacks of him hitting a long-distance headshot of his family's murderer, who was driving a moving vehicle, a 1200-yard killshot, from a file read by Director Leon Vance in the episode "Deliverance" and in "Jeopardy" he hits a kidnapper with a very swift killshot in the forehead - he takes this shot while kneeling from inside a car trunk, with

his left hand. In "Truth or Consequences", Gibbs saved his entire team by shooting the leader of a terrorist cell with a killshot after DiNozzo and McGee get captured looking for Ziva after she quits NCIS.
Gibbs is one of three characters to have appeared in every episode.

Source: [1]

Gibbs' Rules

Rule #1:   Never let suspects stay together.

Rule #2:   Always wear gloves at a crime scene.

Rule #3:   Don't believe what you're told. Double check.

Rule #3:   Never be unreachable. (Rule #3 double-used)

Rule #4:   If you have a secret, the best thing is to keep it to yourself. The second-best is to tell one other person if you must. There is no third best.

Rule #5:   You don't waste good.

Rule #6:   Never say you're sorry. It's a sign of weakness.

Rule #7:   Always be specific when you lie.

Rule #8:   Never take anything for granted.

Rule #9:   Never go anywhere without a knife.

Rule #10:   Never get personally involved in a case.

Rule #11:   When the job is done, walk away.

Rule #12:   Never date a coworker.

Rule #13:   Never, ever involve lawyers.

Rule #15:   Always work as a team.

Rule #16:   If someone thinks they have the upper hand, break
            it.

Rule #18:   It's better to ask forgiveness than ask permission.

Rule #22:   Never, ever interrupt Gibbs in interrogation.

Rule #23:   Never mess with a Marine's coffee if you want to
            live.

Rule #27:   There are two ways to follow someone.
            1st way - they never notice you
            2nd way - they only notice you.

Rule #35:   Always watch the watchers.

Rule #36:   If it feels like you're being played, you probably
            are.

Rule #38:   Your case, your lead.

Rule #39:   There is no such thing as coincidence.

Rule #40:   If it seems like someone's out to get you, they are.

Rule #44:   First things first, hide the women and children.

Rule #45:   Clean up your messes.

Rule #51:   Sometimes - you're wrong.

Source: [2]

Name: Anthony D. DiNozzo

Occupation: Special agent, Major Case Response
                            Team Senior Field Agent, NCIS,
                            Former Detective (BPD)

Gender: Male

Nationality: American, Italian descent

Family: Anthony D. DiNozzo Sr. (father)
                            Unnamed mother

Source: [1]

Senior Special Agent Anthony "Tony" D. DiNozzo, portrayed by
Michael Weatherly, is a former homicide detective for the
Baltimore Police Department. Prior to Baltimore, he worked for
Philadelphia PD and Peoria PD. Like Gibbs, has a limited
patience for the scientific method and technical terms. DiNozzo
is perhaps best known for his seemingly-endless film
references; Ziva insists that his dying words will be "I've
seen this film". He attended Ohio State University as a
physical education major and was a member of the "Alpha Chi
Delta" fraternity, class of 1989. DiNozzo is said to have
played college basketball, "running the point for Ohio State"
according to Abby Sciuto in a discussion with her assistant,
Chip. It is mentioned that he comes from a wealthy family but
was disowned by his father, Anthony DiNozzo Sr, played by
Robert Wagner who in turn was played by Weatherly in a TV
movie. DiNozzo's mother was over-protective, and she "dressed
him like a sailor until he was ten."
He is a flirt, and has had his fair share of success in that
department. He has a fondness for playing pranks on his co-
workers and little respect for their boundaries. During the
course of the fourth season, he was on an undercover assignment
that Director Jenny Shepard led, the key mission being to find
arms dealer La Grenouille by posing as La Grenouille's
daughter's boyfriend, but ended up falling in love with her. In
the episode "Knockout", he revealed that he was not doing well
with women and that he was still hurting from his relationship
with Jeanne Benoit. There is a great deal of romantic tension
between Tony and Ziva. Despite his playboy manner and light-
hearted nature, DiNozzo is frequently shown to be very sharp;
he is able to coax Mossad Director Eli David into admitting
that he ordered Rivkin and Ziva to spy on NCIS.
Reassigned as an Agent Afloat in Season 5 ("Judgment Day")
Transferred back to the Major Case Response Team in Season 6
("Agent Afloat"). DiNozzo is one of three characters to have
appeared in every episode.

Source: [1]

Name: Caitlin Todd(†)

Occupation: Special Agent, Major Case Response
Team Field Agent, (NCIS)
Former Special Agent, (USSS)

Gender: Female

Family: Rachel Cranston (older sister)
Three Unnamed brothers

Caitlin Todd, portrayed by Sasha Alexander, first appeared in
the episode "Yankee White". Todd was a former Secret Service
agent, recruited by Gibbs after she successfully helped him
solve a murder aboard Air Force One.

She worked well with everyone on the team, becoming
particularly close with Ducky and Abby, who convinced her to
get a tattoo (referenced in the episode "Kill Ari (Part 1)").
Her relationship with Gibbs is unique, as there appeared to be
a real friendship between the two characters; which is unusual
considering Gibbs is not a close friend with anyone.

Her relationship with Tony, however, was more adversarial and
appeared to be more of siblings than anything else. Tony
frequently flirted with her and went through her personal
belongings, no matter how many times she pointed out that his
behavior was grossly unprofessional. At the same time, Kate is
willing to risk her life for DiNozzo and admits that life would
be considerably less interesting without him around.

Todd was killed in the line of duty at the end of the episode
"Twilight" by Ari Haswari, collateral damage in the terrorist's
obsession with Gibbs. She received a fatal gunshot wound to the
head from a sniper rifle fired by Ari Haswari. Todd also made
appearances in "Kill Ari" parts 1 and 2 as a hallucination,
remembered by her teammates.

She was replaced at NCIS by Israeli Mossad Liaison Officer Ziva
David

Source: ¹

Name: Ziva David

Occupation:

2009-present. Special agent. Major Case Response Team Field Agent. NCIS (Season 7-present). 2005-2009 Mossad Liaison Officer (with NCIS) (seasons 3-7. 2003-2005 Mossad operative. control officer. 2001-2003 Soldier in the Israeli Army

Gender:

Female

Family:

Eli David (father) Rivka David (mother. deceased). Ari Haswari paternal half brother. (deceased) Tali David (sister. deceased)

Ziva David. portrayed by Cote de Pablo. formerly held the post of Mossad Liaison Officer to NCIS. to which she was appointed following the murder of Special Agent Caitlin Todd by a rogue Mossad operative named Ari Haswari. Ziva was Ari's control officer and half-sister. After Agent Todd's death. she requested a liaison assignment to NCIS. where she subsequently joined Special Agent Leroy Jethro Gibbs' team. At the end of Season 6. Ziva falls under suspicion as a spy for the Mossad.

Her specialty with the Mossad was espionage. assassination and terrorism and is highly trained in the martial arts. She speaks Hebrew. English. Arabic. Spanish. French. Italian. German Title. Russian and Turkish. Despite being fluent in English. she sometimes misinterprets idioms and phrases that have different meanings in other languages if translated directly; this is a running joke within the series.

Ziva is very skilled with a knife and has been shown teaching her colleagues how to throw it properly. She is the one person Gibbs trusts with any type of firearm in difficult. potentially hazardous. situations.

In her career. she has traveled extensively to countries including Egypt (where she met Jenny Shepard). Iraq. the United Kingdom and Morocco.

In the episode "Good Cop, Bad Cop" Ziva became a probationary NCIS Special Agent after she terminated her links with Mossad for good. Since then, Tony has referred to her (as with McGee) as "Probie". As of "Rule Fifty-One", she is a citizen of the United States and able to become a full agent which is made official in Season 9's "Nature of the Beast".

Ziva rarely speaks of her personal life. Her father Eli David is the director of Mossad. The show rarely mentions Ziva's mother, Rivka, who taught her to drive; all that is known is that she does not have the same mother as Ari.

Her younger sister, Talia "Tali" David, was killed in a Hamas terrorist attack against Israel at the age of sixteen. She also has an Aunt Nettie who likes to play mahjong.

Ziva's hobbies include playing the piano, singing, dancing (she took ballet when she was young), cooking, reading, and boxing. She enjoys the fictional drink Berry Mango Madness.

She drives a red Mini Cooper, likes listening to the Israeli band Hadag Nachash and the Latin American band Kinky. She does not own a television but her favorite film is The Sound of Music.

De Pablo describes the character as someone who is "completely different from anyone else on the show" and that because "she's been around men all her life; she's used to men in authority. She's not afraid of men."

Source: [1]

Name: Timothy McGee

Occupation:	Special agent, Major Case Response Team Field Agent, NCIS (Seasons 2-Present), Norfolk Case Agent and Major Case Response Team TAD Field Agent, NCIS (Season 1)
Gender:	Male
Family:	Sarah McGee (Sister) Penelope Langston (Grandmother)

Timothy McGee, portrayed by Sean Murray, first appeared in the episode "Sub Rosa" as a Case Agent stationed at Norfolk, and was promoted to Field Agent and assigned to Agent Gibbs' team in the second season, becoming a regular character, where he became a Junior Special Agent with NCIS. He serves as a field computer consultant and occasionally assists Abby Sciuto in the lab.

He clashes with DiNozzo, though after the two became partners (following Ziva's departure from the team at the end of season six), they are frequently shown to form an effective team; however, once Ziva returns, their relationship reverts to its original state. McGee's methods are often indecipherable to the other team members, have earned him the pejorative nickname "McGeek" and "McGoo" (along with other derisive nicknames based on his surname), as well as "Probie", and "Elf Lord", the latter used by multiple characters due to his elf character in an online role playing computer game. He was trained in biomedical engineering at Johns Hopkins University, and computer forensics at Massachusetts Institute of Technology (MIT). He also graduated the top of his class at the Federal Law Enforcement Training Center.

McGee is also a writer, writing mystery crime novels including a national best seller, Deep Six, under the pseudonym Thom E. Gemcity (an anagram of his name), featuring characters based on his fellow co-workers and others from his everyday life. He also drives a silver Porsche Boxster as seen in the episode "Twisted Sister". He has Apple's iPhone smartphone, and uses it frequently on investigation. He owns a dog named Jethro. Jethro was in a prior episode where he had been falsely accused of killing his police handler. Abby proved his innocence, named him Jethro and had to convince McGee to take Jethro because her landlord wouldn't let her keep the dog. ("Dog Tags") McGee was transferred to Cybercrimes Division in Season 5 ("Judgment Day") and back to the Major Case Response Team in Season 6 ("Last Man Standing").

Source: [1]

Name: Abigail Sciuto

Occupation: Forensic Specialist, NCIS

Gender: Female

Religion: Catholic

Abigail "Abby" Sciuto, portrayed by Pauley Perrette, is a forensic specialist with NCIS. As indicated in the episode "Seadog", she is the child of deaf parents. She is known for her gothic style of dress and addiction to the fictional, high-caffeine beverage "Caf-Pow". Abby had a brief sexual relationship with Special Agent McGee, as seen in the episode "Reveille" in season one, which ended with the two remaining friends.

She is the most active and affectionate person of the team, often hugging everyone and talking fast, though she can be easily distracted. She is one of the few who can talk to Gibbs freely, and he often buys her Caf-Pow. She and Gibbs are both fluent in sign language. She has a stuffed farting hippopotamus named Bert that often appears in the show.

Abby developed a fondness for a Navy sniffer dog in the season 5 episode "Dog Tags". Originally named "Butch", she renamed it "Jethro" (after Gibbs) for being "handsome and quiet". The dog was framed for the murder of a petty officer, but Abby proves Jethro's innocence. Afterwards, Abby forces McGee to adopt him, much to his dismay (as Jethro had attacked him earlier in the episode). Abby would have preferred to adopt Jethro herself, but was prohibited from doing so by her landlord.

Abby's hobbies include a bowling league with nuns, helping build homes for the needy, and playing computer games. She also sleeps in a coffin and is, according to DiNozzo, "the happiest goth you will ever meet."

Abby is one of three characters to have appeared in every episode and like Director Leon Vance, also appears on the spin-off series, NCIS Los Angeles.

Source: [1]

Name: Dr.Donald Mallard

Occupation: Chief Medical Examiner

Gender: Male

Dr. Donald "Ducky" Mallard, portrayed by David McCallum, is the Chief Medical Examiner at NCIS. Dr. Mallard is a Scottish-born doctor, who has been long-time friends with Gibbs, and underwent medical education at the University of Edinburgh Medical School, and served in the Royal Army Medical Corps. He has a "second talent", as Gibbs calls it, to be able to read people, which he expands in Season 4 by studying psychology. In cases without actual bodies, he assists by using his psychological training to decipher the clues left by the perpetrators. Dr. Mallard is an eccentric character who often talks to the deceased and rambles to the living with many long personal remembrances or historical accounts, but is a kind man at heart. He also calls co-workers by their full first names (ex: Abigail instead of Abby)—with the exceptions of Gibbs and medical assistant Jimmy Palmer, whom he addresses as Jethro and Mr. Palmer, respectively (although he does refer to Palmer by his first name, Jimmy, when concerned for him, as revealed in About Face). Although most of his time is spent in autopsy and going to crime scenes to examine bodies, he was sent on a highly important undercover mission in the episode "Blowback". He also spent some time in Afghanistan during the Soviet invasion, and in Bosnia during the Balkan conflict.
Ducky and Gibbs have worked together for many years. When Gibbs was asked, "What did Ducky look like when he was younger?" he replied, "Illya Kuryakin"—the Russian spy played by McCallum in the 1960s television show The Man From U.N.C.L.E. Ducky drives a Morgan that he restored himself. In the episode "Hung Out to Dry," it is revealed that he has a nephew, though no further information follows. The ring tone on his cell phone features bagpipes playing "Scotland the Brave".
He lived with his aging mother and her corgi dogs until season 6. In the episode "Broken Bird", Ducky revealed his mother had moved out and had Alzheimer's disease. Nina Foch, the actress who played Ducky's mother, died on December 5, 2008, necessitating the change. In the episode "Double Identity", it was revealed Ducky's mother had died. Her headstone indicated 1912-2010. The rest of the team only learns of Victoria Mallard's passing when Abby follows Ducky to her gravesite. Later Gibbs pays him a condolence call in the autopsy room, but Ducky seems relieved at her death rather than sad (probably that she was no longer suffering from Alzheimer's), and grateful to have been her son.He expresses to Gibbs his pride at the fact that she had almost lived to the age of 100.

Source: '

Name: Jimmy Palmer

Occupation: Medical Examiner Assistant

Gender: Male

Jim (Jimmy) Palmer, portrayed by Brian Dietzen, and sometimes referred to by Tony as "Autopsy Gremlin", first appeared in the episode "Split Decision". After Gerald Jackson was incapacitated, Palmer became Mallard's medical assistant both in the field and in the morgue. In the episode "About Face", Jimmy became a central character of the episode who must recover his memory to find a suspect to the murder case and his attempted killer. He self-identifies as a sufferer of a "mild" case of diabetes mellitus in the episode "In The Dark". He is terrified of Gibbs. Part of the reason that Doctor Mallard and he are often not at the crime scene until well after Gibbs and his team arrive is related to Dr. Mallard's emphasis on Jimmy being a horrible driver and always getting lost, although Jimmy tries to defend himself by pointing out that Ducky is the one with the map. He was named after former Baltimore Orioles pitcher Jim Palmer, but does not like baseball.

In many of the episodes, Jimmy is seen fraternizing with Michelle Lee. Often they make excuses for working late and are seen entering and exiting the underside of the autopsy table. In the episode "Last Man Standing", Palmer admits to Gibbs and Vance that he and Agent Lee had been "doing it" for a while. In the episode "The Good Wives Club" it is revealed that Jimmy is claustrophobic; when he is entering the enclosed hallway he is seen sweating profusely and when he has to go get the body bag he gets freaked out about having to go back through it.

In the episode "About Face", as Jimmy was being hypnotized by Abby, it can be inferred that he has a foot/shoe fetish as he dreamily states in great detail about Ziva and Abby's footwear, instead of recalling information about the current case. The episode also leads us to believe that his mother's name is Eunice. In the episode "Bounce" it is shown that Palmer regularly helped Tony when he was in charge. Jimmy Palmer is also shown to have severe tinnitus.

In season 7 it was revealed that Jimmy was in love with a girl named Breena Slater, who appeared in the episode "Mother's Day". In the season 8 finale "Pyramid", NCIS special agent E.J. Barrett congratulates Jimmy with his engagement. *Source:* [1]

Name: Jennifer Shepard(†)

Occupation: NCIS Director

Gender: Female

Jenny Shepard, portrayed by Lauren Holly, first appeared in the episode "Kill Ari (Part 1)". She replaced former NCIS director Thomas Morrow, at the start of the third season after Morrow took a Deputy Director's position with the Department of Homeland Security. She is also a "military brat" as her father Colonel Jasper Shepard was an Army officer.

She was Gibbs' former partner and former lover. While she and Gibbs were stationed in Europe, Gibbs was ordered back to the States and she was offered her own section in Europe. When Gibbs asked Jenny to go with him, she refused. They were reunited in "Kill Ari (Part 1)" which stirred Gibbs' heart, and opened a constant flirtation between her and Gibbs. Jenny was killed in the episode "Judgment Day (Part 1)". At the time of her death she was already dying from a terminal illness that was never specified. Only she, Ducky, and Mike Franks ever knew, and Ducky broke the truth to Gibbs after her passing.

Shepard had a close relationship with Ziva David and occasionally provided her with key information on a case without going through regular channels or telling Gibbs, as in the Season 3 episode "Head Case." They made it a point to keep these dealings confidential; "What Gibbs doesn't know can't hurt us," Shepard quipped. Later in the episode, though, Gibbs' remarks revealed that he knew about her assistance. Shepard and Ziva had a working relationship prior Shepard being appointed Director of NCIS.

During season 4, Director Shepard places Tony DiNozzo on an undercover assignment to get close to notorious international arms dealer René Benoit, otherwise known as La Grenouille. The sub-plot comes to a head late in the season when it is revealed that she blames Benoit for the death of her father and that Benoit is now central to a major CIA deep-cover operation.

Gibbs confronts her over the operation, suggesting that Shepard is letting her emotions dictate her actions and that she has knowingly placed DiNozzo in danger and jeopardized a major CIA operation for the purposes of getting revenge, while hiding behind her position as NCIS director to justify her actions. During the episode "Internal Affairs", it is strongly implied that Shepard was responsible for the murder of La Grenouille, something reiterated when Gibbs looks through the FBI's file on the death of La Grenouille in "Judgement Day (Part 1)".

In several episodes during season five, before her death in the episode "Judgement Day (Part 1)", her failing health becomes a plot issue, as for example when Ducky is shown to be ordering a test on a blood sample to Abby, telling her that it is from a John Doe. However, when Abby talks to Jimmy Palmer, he says that they have no John Does. Gibbs deduces, correctly, that the only person Ducky would act this way for would be the Director, at the end of the episode "Stakeout". In the next episode "Dog Tags", Gibbs questions Jenny about her illness and she lies to him, saying she is fine. It is never revealed as to what was killing her.

Mike Franks also discovers her illness by going through her purse and finding her medication. In the episode "Judgment Day (Part 1)", Franks and Jenny are talking in an abandoned diner in the California desert and she indicates that she is dying and reveals that she regrets her decision to leave Gibbs in Paris and that she is still in love with him. It is revealed that she botched an operation ten years prior where she and Gibbs had been ordered to assassinate Russian lovers who were crime lords.

Gibbs shot the man, but Jenny faced the woman, Natasha (AKA Svetlana), down and let her live. As a result, Natasha sends assassins who kill Jenny in the diner but only after Jenny manages to kill all of them. Franks, who had been outside at the time of the shooting, returns to Jenny's house where Natasha is trying to kill Gibbs and Franks shoots her.

Gibbs and Franks decide to cover Jenny's mistake and death by burning down her Georgetown mansion and her cause of death is reported as "death in home fire". Her death rattles the crew and makes them all depressed. Abby regrets that she never told Jenny she was a snappy dresser, and says that would have made her smile.

After Director Shepard's death, she was replaced by Assistant Director Leon Vance.

Source: [1]

Name: Leon Vance

Occupation: NCIS Director

Gender: Male

Leon Vance, portrayed by Rocky Carroll, first appeared in the episode "Internal Affairs" as Assistant Director in Season 5. He is named Director after the death of Jenny Shepard. It has been revealed in the episode "Knockout" that he was originally from Ohio, but grew up in Chicago where he trained to be a boxer. In this episode, his wife stated that Vance attended the United States Naval Academy and was commissioned as a 2nd Lieutenant in the Marine Corps, but was forced to take a medical discharge before ever serving due to having undergone surgery to repair a detached retina suffered during his boxing career.

However, at the end of the episode, Ducky reveals to Gibbs that Vance's close, childhood friend who had died just prior to the start of the episode also suffered a detached retina. In the course of this episode, Vance also revealed that it was this friend who decided that Vance should leave Chicago while the friend stayed behind. Vance said this despite his insistence to Gibbs that his friend was a Marine though there was no record of his friend's service in the military.

In 1991, just prior to joining NCIS, Vance was a student at the United States Naval War College in Rhode Island. His coursework at this time included Combat Philosophy and Advanced Cryptography. It was during his time at the War College that he began to take an interest in black operations and even imagined one himself: Operation Frankenstein, which would later play a big part in the season 8 finale.

NIS took an interest in him and he was hired for an operation by Special Agent Whitney Sharp for an operation in Amsterdam codenamed Trident. Vance was trained by Sharp and left after a six-week training course for Amsterdam where he met his handler, Riley McAllister. McAllister told him that the target of the operation was a Russian intelligence operative who was known to Vance only as the Russian. NIS believed that he was bribing sailors in return for intelligence. Vance later met Eli David, a promising agent of the Mossad, who told him that he knew of the operation and that the Russian would kill him. Later, Eli betrayed Vance to the Russian but it was revealed that it was so that he would try to kill Vance sooner so that he could kill him himself. Eli also told Vance that he had been chosen because he was expendable and that he wasn't someone who would be missed.

Eli and Vance kill the Russian's hit team but the Russian manages to escape and Eli is unable to find him or who he was for that matter. Vance was credited for the elimination of the hit team and he started to rise swiftly through the ranks at NCIS. He kept believing along with Eli, that Amsterdam was not what it had seemed and they came to the conclusion that there was a dirty agent in NCIS, the one who had really tipped off the Russian of Vance's mission. It was later revealed that McAllister had masterminded the entire operation: being an expert in Russia, he had seen that the Soviet Union's collapse had laid attention away from Russia and onto the Middle East. Knowing that new attention to a potential Russian threat would throw him in the spotlight for Director of NIS, he had planned to have Vance killed by a Russian operative so as to show that Russia still posed a threat and so that he could satisfy his ambitions.

Notably, Vance took over for Jenny Shepard during her leave of absence between "Internal Affairs" and "Judgment Day," establishing himself as a formidable presence with Gibbs and his team. He and Gibbs clash during this span, prompting a cold war between them which ends with a détente between the two of them in "Agent Afloat" at the start of the sixth season; however, the two of them clash later on, as Gibbs feels he cannot fully trust Vance, though he cannot identify a specific reason why.

Vance spearheads the investigation into Jenny Shepard's death, and is angered greatly when he is not kept in the loop by Gibbs and Mike Franks, who ultimately manipulate the situation to exonerate Shepard from her past failure, not what Vance had in mind. After Shepard's death, and possibly before, he lobbies the Secretary of the Navy hard to take over NCIS, as told in "Cloak," but in "Semper Fidelis" the Secretary of the Navy informs Gibbs of a major operation which will require Vance to serve as its head, and that NCIS and the Navy will need Gibbs and Vance to get along, to which Gibbs is not comfortable but appreciates the situation.

Things come to a head in "Aliyah," when Gibbs accuses Vance of selling out his team to Mossad Director Eli David, to which Vance responds that Ziva was a plant, used to get Mossad a foothole in NCIS through Gibbs. After this, the two of them realize that circumstances will prove one of them right.

At the start of the seventh season, Vance approves Ziva's transfer to NCIS, proving that Gibbs was right, and Ziva was loyal to NCIS. Despite his professional attitude towards Gibbs's team, he shows that he does care about them at least once when Alejandro Rivera threatens Abby in "Spider and The Fly". He tells Alejandro to leave before he gets hurt and when Alejandro asks by who, he replies angrily: "By me."

Even after the events of "Aliyah," Vance has been shown to still be in official contact with Eli David in David's capacity as Director of Mossad. This is shown when he receives a text message on his phone from Eli which says only: "I found him".

Vance also refuses to discuss an Eli-phone call with Gibbs, despite knowing how dangerous Eli is, and his precarious relationship with Gibbs and his team.

Upon being promoted to the director's position at the end of Season 5, Vance immediately goes to former Director Shepard's office, and is seen to shred a single mysterious document from his own personnel file. It is later revealed in season 6 ("Semper Fidelis") that the document was written by his supervising agent at the time. The Secretary of the Navy tells Gibbs that the file is a fabrication and that he thought all copies had been destroyed. It is further revealed in the season 8 episode, "Enemies Domestic", that the head of the San Diego field office, when Vance was assigned there, had begun creating a legend for Vance that incorporated fictitious information about Vance in order to backstop a deep cover assignment, including the false information that Vance had been a pilot and director of a field office.

Leon Vance has a wife, Jackie, and two children, a daughter, Kayla, and a son, Jared. He met his wife while attending a University of Maryland basketball game while Len Bias was playing.

Vance is also a recurring character on the NCIS spin-off, NCIS Los Angeles.

Source: 1

Spin-off

The concept and characters were initially introduced in a two-part episode of the CBS series JAG (JAG episodes 8.20 and 8.21). The show, a spin-off from JAG, premiered on September 23, 2003 on CBS and, to date, has aired eight full seasons and has gone into syndicated reruns on USA Network, Cloo (formerly Sleuth) and Ion Television. Donald Bellisario, who created JAG as well as the well-known series Airwolf, Magnum, P.I. and Quantum Leap, is co-creator and executive producer of NCIS.

Source: [1]

Season 1 (Episodes 1.1- 1.23)

Originally broadcast between September 23, 2003 and May 25, 2004, the first season essentially dealt with introducing the characters and their strengths, skills and weaknesses. It also introduced the main foe for the first two seasons, Ari Haswari, two recurring characters in the form of Timothy McGee and Jimmy Palmer after Gerald Jackson, Ducky's assistant, was shot, and Special Agent Caitlin Todd as Special Agent Vivian Blackadder's replacement.

Source: [1]

Original Air Date USA   September 23, 2003 – May 25, 2004 on CBS

Original Air Date German Language   March 17, 2005 – August 25, 2005 on Sat 1

Episodes Season 1

No.	German Title	US Title	Air Date USA	Air Date GER	Directed by	Written by
1.1	Air Force One	**Yankee White**	Sep 23, 2003	Mar 17, 2005	D.Bellisario	D.Bellisario & D.McGill

While on Air Force One, a Navy Commander tasked with carrying the "football" dies under mysterious circumstances, forcing an emergency landing in Wichita, Kansas but while his death is originally thought be to a tragic accident, NCIS eventually uncovers evidence suggesting the Commander was murdered and that it might be connected to a possible assassination attempt on the President. *Source:* [1]

Gibbs Rule #1: Never let suspects stay together.
Gibbs Rule #2: Always wear gloves at a crime scene.
Gibbs Rule #3: Never believe what your told always double check.

Kate: I can't give him Air Force One's floor plans, they're top secret!
Gibbs: Come on, Agent Todd. I saw all this in a Harrison Ford movie.
Gibbs: NCIS does not leak. These plans get out... you can shoot DiNozzo.
Kate: No, I think I'm destined to shoot you.

Gibbs: Please?
Abby: Wow! Gibbs said "Please".

Gibbs: Don't believe what you're told. Always double check.
Kate: Should I write these on my Palm Pilot, or crochet them on pillows?

Gibbs: I heard you quit, Agent Todd.
Kate: Happy news gets around fast. Yes, I resigned. It was the right thing to do.
Gibbs: Yep. Pull that crap at NCIS, I won't give you a chance to resign.
Kate: Is that a job offer?
(Tony is in an FBI van in a body bag, pretending to be a dead body)
Tony: Hello?
Gibbs: We're in the clear.You can get out of the body bag.
Tony: I never thought I'd say this, but I'm not sure I want to.
GIbbs: What? You gotta search Commander Trapp's apartment tonight.
Tony: Aw, Gibbs, come'on.It's one am.
Gibbs: Agent Axelrod is tailing you to pick up the bag when the FBI tosses it.
Tony: That's funny, Gibbs, real funny.....Gah!
Gibbs: I guess they found him.

Kate: I may not know the finer points of investigating, like sticking needles in liver and measuring swimsuit models, but I do know enough to hold the stewards who prepared and served the President's lunch.
Gibbs: Hum. Okay.
Kate: You want to question them?
Gibbs: No, they're not going anywhere, and we've got a crime scene to investigate. Rule Number One. Never let suspects stay together.
Kate: Well, I didn't consider them suspects.
Gibbs: Then why'd you hold them?

Tony: Tell me her measurements.
Kate: You're pathetic.Tony: No, I'm serious. Can you tell if she's five foot four and a thirty-four C, or five foot seven and a thirty-six D? You can't. Not from a photo. That's why we do sketches and take measurements. Thank you.

Source: [3]

Episodes Season 1

No.	German Title	US Title	Air Date USA	Air Date GER	Directed by	Written by
1.2	Sprung in den Tod	**Hung Out to Dry**	Sep 30, 2003	Mar 31, 2005	A.Levi	D.McGill

A Marine dies during a night-time training jump. The culprit seems to be a faulty parachute, but the standard investigation reveals that the death might not have been an accident after all. Gibbs begins to believe that the supposed accident which resulted in the Marine's death may actually be murder and he, Tony and Kate set out to find out who tampered with the dead Marine's faulty parachute and eventually sent him unknowingly to his death.
Source: [1]

Tony: Ducky? Why would Gibbs rip his hard line out and dunk his cell phone in a jar of paint thinner?
Ducky: Oh, dear.
Tony: What?
Ducky: Oh, I should have realized the time of year. It's his anniversary.
Tony: Which marriage?
Ducky: Well, the last one, of course.
Tony: Ducky. I'm not following.
Ducky: Every year, ex-wife number three gets drunk on their anniversary and calls him repeatedly.
Tony: Why doesn't he, ah, change his number?
Ducky: No idea. In case you haven't noticed, Gibbs is a man of more questions than answers.

Gibbs: Only thing you can use the DNA registry for is to identify a body.
Kate: Well, there has to be a way around that.
Gibbs: See? Now you're thinking like an NCIS agent.

Gibbs: *(referring to the boots)* Put 'em on. Can't work a field in high heels.
Tony: Depends on the kind of work you're doing.
Kate: Your mind, DiNozzo, runs the gamut from X to XXX.
Tony: Yeah?

Tony: Very electric Kool-Aid, Abby.
Abby: I was thinking more Blue Man Group.
Tony: Wow, why didn't you take to me this fast?
Abby: You're like a piercing, Tony. It takes a while for the throbbing to stop and the skin to grow back.
Tony: That's more than I wanted to know.

Kate: How did you get into NCIS?
Tony: I smiled.
Kate: How'd you get into this?
Abby: Filled out an application.

Tony: Do you jump?
Gibbs: Only when I get an electric shock.
Tony: That explains the lack of power tools.
Gibbs: So you gonna do it?
Tony: What?
Gibbs: Spend $180 to defy gravity?
Tony: *(grinning)* Yeah, I think I am.
Gibbs: Y'know, some of these guys freeze on their first jump. Have to be kicked in the ass to get them out.
Tony: Not me.
Gibbs: Nope. You fall in the category of want to get kicked in the ass on the ground.

Source: [3]

Episodes Season 1

No.	German Title	US Title	Air Date USA	Air Date GER	Directed by	Written by
1.3	Seadog	**Seadog**	Oct 7, 2003	Apr 7, 2005	B.May	D.Bellisario & J.Kelley

When a Naval Commander is murdered, seemingly during a freelance drugs deal gone sour, the media is quick to link him to drug trafficking and the evidence stacks up. Being a former Marine himself, Gibbs refuses to believe that a good officer could be so corrupt, and in his efforts to clear the Commander's record and good name, uncovers a turf war between two rival drug gangs, and a terrorist's scheme to knock out the national power grid. The NCIS team is aided in its investigation by the DEA, and FBI Special Agent Tobias Fornell. *Source: [1]*

```
Gerald: You shoved a French cop over a cliff?
Ducky: There was a lake below.
Gibbs: Sixty feet below!

Kate: I did work for the Secret Service. We tend to get all hot and bothered
over large sums of $100 bills.
Tony: Is that what does it for you?
Kate: What does it for me, Tony, is a mystery that you will never solve.
```
Source: [3]

No.	German Title	US Title	Air Date USA	Air Date GER	Directed by	Written by
1.4	Die Unsterblichen	**The Immortals**	Oct 14, 2003	Apr 14, 2005	A.Levi	D.Meyers

The discovery of a drowned sailor in dress whites, with an officer's ceremonial sword and weights chained to his waist, sparks a suicide investigation and eventually sends the team to the USS Foster so that they can dig into the deceased officer's life and find out what his colleagues thought of him. Kate refuses to believe that the deceased sailor committed suicide, as like her, he came from a Catholic family where suicide is a mortal sin. Meanwhile Abby discovers a link between the crew of the USS Foster and an MMORPG known as 'The Immortals', and begins searching the game for clues and evidence in order to assist Gibbs in solving the case and saving the ship from possible destruction. *Source: [1]*

```
Tony: Aren't you guys interested at all in what I brought you back from Puerto
Rico?
Gibbs/Kate: (sighing) Sure. Fine. (Tony grins and hands them a couple bags, Kate looks in hers)
Kate: You gotta be kidding.
Tony: A bikini. Two-piece.
Kate: A bottom. And a hat?
Tony: Puerto Rican!
Gibbs: Any chance you're going to try that on?
Kate: (tosses it at Gibbs) You first.
Gibbs: (looks over the bikini bottom) Trust me. It's not gonna fit.
Kate: Pigs. I work with pigs.
Tony: (as Gibbs is opening his gift) It's a fantasy RPG book. Complete with character sheets
and dice. Baby steps, Gibbs. Baby steps.
Gibbs: It's in Spanish.
Tony: There's just no pleasing you, is there?
```
Source: [3]

Episodes Season 1

No.	German Title	US Title	Air Date USA	Air Date GER	Directed by	Written by
1.5	Der Fluch der Mumie	**The Curse**	Oct 28, 2003	Apr 21, 2005	T.O'Hara	Bellisario,McGill&Vlaming

Gibbs and the team are called in when a mummified lieutenant, who was believed to have absconded with 1.2 million dollars of stolen Navy funds ten years previously, is found in a half-buried cargo pod with Navy markings on it. Two former shipmates who serve with the deceased come under suspicion for both the murder and the theft. Gibbs and Tony work at investigating the murder, while Kate is charged with tracking down the missing funds. Abby uses a computer reconstruction to work a confession out of a possible suspect. *Source: [1]*

```
Gibbs: Tony you gas the truck
Tony: Uh Gibbs you know most agencies have people who do that sort of thing.
Gibbs: Uh huh...so do we.

Tony: I didn't become an NCIS agent yesterday Kate. As a matter of fact
tomorrow...
Gibbs: ...is going to be two years.
Tony: That's kind of touching Gibbs. Remembering the day you hired me.
Gibbs: Yeah, well it seemed like a good idea at the time.

Gibbs: That tank came off a Tomcat. Somebody filed a TFOA report.
Kate: TFOA?
Tony: Things Falling Off Aircraft.
Kate: You're kidding.
Gibbs: Nope, that's what they're called.
```

Source: [3]

No.	German Title	US Title	Air Date USA	Air Date GER	Directed by	Written by
1.6	Speed	**High Seas**	Nov 4, 2003	Apr 28, 2005	D.Smith	L.Moskowitz & J.Vlaming

One of Gibbs's former team members, NCIS Special Agent Stan Burley (Joel Gretsch) who is Agent Afloat on the USS Enterprise calls for assistance when a sailor suffers a meth overdose while on leave, despite the sailor in question claiming that he's never taken the drug. When another sailor is admitted to sickbay under the same circumstances, Tony and Kate investigate the source of the drugs within the crew while Gibbs begins to suspect that a senior officer on the ship may secretly be doping the crew with performance-enhancing drugs. *Source: [1]*

```
Tony: Five years with Gibbs? Amazed the guy didn't end up in a straitjacket.
Gibbs: What was that?
Tony: Uh, nothing, Boss, just praising your communication skills.

Gibbs: Above his mattress, below his mattress, inside his mattress. If there's
such a thing as a fourth mattress dimension, go over that, too.

Tony: Is this going to turn into one of those guy-girl things where you insist
we stop and ask for directions?

Abby: Smart money says that that is not a Tic-Tac.

Gibbs: That pouch may be clear, but my gut is still in living color.

Tony: I say it's time we turn out the lights and play in the dark.
```

Source: [3]

Episodes Season 1

No.	German Title	US Title	Air Date USA	Air Date GER	Directed by	Written by
1.7	Unter Wasser	**Sub Rosa**	Nov 18, 2003	Mar 24, 2005	M.Zinberg	F.Cardea & G.Schenck

NCIS Norfolk Case Agent Timothy McGee works on a case of a partially dissolved corpse found in a barrel of acid at the Norfolk Naval Base, and calls in the Major Case Response Team to help him. As the investigation continues, it soon becomes apparent that the killer took steps to prevent the body from being identified. Gibbs quickly comes to believe that the motive for the brutal murder was identity theft and his suspicions are further confirmed when it's revealed that although a submariner is dead, no-one has been reported missing, leading Gibbs to believe that an imposter is on one of the submarines. Tony, Abby, and McGee are tasked with identifying the deceased, while Gibbs and Kate are sent underwater on a submarine to vet five possible suspects, one of whom might have been responsible for the murder and also prevent a chemical attack from happening. *Source:* [1]

McGee: I've heard stories about Special Agent Gibbs.
Tony: Only half of them are true. Trick is figuring out which half.

Abby: There's good news and bad news.
Ducky: I hate it when you play this game, Abby. All right, let's get it over with.
Abby: His last meal was a Big Mac and fries.
Ducky: Well, probably half the base had that for lunch. I was hoping you'd come up with something more exotic. Tandoori, perhaps. And the good news?
Abby: I know what's in the special sauce.

Gibbs: Drink.
Kate: What's with all the water?
Gibbs: Oh, you gotta hydrate on a sub marine.
Kate: All you've had me doing is hydrating.
Gibbs: Drink it. *(she takes a drink)* So how's your bladder?
Kate: What?
Gibbs: The COB's at the end of the passageway are trying to keep an eye on us. You gotta distract 'em. *(Kate looks at him)* You're gonna need help working the toilet.
Kate: Gibbs....
Gibbs: Trust me, Kate, on a Sub Marine it's a very complicated mechanism.
Kate: Is that why you've been shoving water down my throat for the past hour?
Gibbs: I wan to check out Petty Officer Thompson.
Kate: Well, you don't have to drown me. You could just ask.
Gibbs: Hydrating good for ya'. Go, unhydrate.
Kate: Never heard it called that before.
Gibbs: Go on.

Tony: Nice hat. Did they make you the boat mascot?
Kate: That's your way of saying you missed me, isn't it?
Tony: No.

Kate: Do people react that way because we're NCIS, or do you just have that effect on them?
Gibbs: I like to think it's me.

Episodes Season 1

No.	German Title	US Title	Air Date USA	Air Date GER	Directed by	Written by
1.8	Schlimmer als der Tod	**Minimum Security**	Nov 25, 2003	May 12, 2005	I.Toynton	D.Bellisario&P.DeGuere

The team heads for Cuba when Ducky and Gerald discover that a dead Guantanamo Bay translator they've been working on has a stomach full of emeralds. NCIS Special Agent Paula Cassidy proves to be more than a match for Tony when he is ordered to investigate her involvement, while Gibbs and Kate try to discover where the emeralds came from, how they ended up in their translator's stomach, and prevent the assassination of an important prisoner. *Source:* [1]

Gibbs: See if you can brand the cologne.
Abby: Why, you want some?
Gibbs: Nope, don't use cologne. Women I date think the smell of sawdust is sexy. Probably why I don't date *(pause)* many women.
Abby: Perfume is the most powerful accessory a woman can wear.
Gibbs: Yeah, well, how much did all this power cost us?
Abby: Around fifteen hundred.
Gibbs: Fifteen hundred dollars?
Abby: Well, not including the tax. I stuck to the thirty most popular scents hoping we'd get lucky.
Gibbs: Ah, how fiscally responsible, Ab.

Source: [3]

No.	German Title	US Title	Air Date USA	Air Date GER	Directed by	Written by
1.9	Anruf von einem Toten	**Marine Down**	Dec 16, 2003	May 19, 2005	D.Smith	J.Kelley

When a dead Marine seemingly calls his wife on the day of his funeral, Gibbs, Tony and Kate begin investigating. The case quickly becomes complicated, as the Marine's CO apparently has two physical forms, and Tony somehow manages to meet and interrogate the victim's wife in a park without even leaving the office. As the investigation continues, the Marine turns up embalmed, having been killed two days after his funeral supposedly took place. Gibbs suspects CIA involvement, and is soon tracking a rogue operative in an attempt to rescue the deceased Marine's partner before another murder takes place. *Source:* [1]

Kate: Gibbs can be wrong sometimes.
Tony: Name once?
Kate: Tony, the man has been married like four times.
Tony: There is that.
Gibbs: There's what, DiNozzo?

Tony, Gibbs, Kate on Military Plane:
Tony: What are you looking for Kate?
Kate: Um the ladies room? *(Gibbs and Tony look at Kate.)*
Kate: Okay, the men's room.
Gibbs: There is no men's room.
Kate: Well then where am I supposed to go to the bathroom?
(Gibbs takes out a white plastic bag and gives it to her. Kate looks disgusted, decides she can wait. Finally gives up and snatches the bag from Gibbs.)
Kate: ****. Where?
Gibbs: Well, if you want some privacy, you can go down behind those boxes.
Kate: God, I miss Air Force One.

Gibbs: Morning! Sleep well?
Kate: If by well, you mean violently throwing up all night and bouncing around like rag dolls...
Tony: Then yeah, boss, we slept very well, thanks for asking.
Gibbs: Ah, you get used to it.
Kate: That's what I'm afraid of.

Source: [3]

Episodes Season 1

No.	German Title	US Title	Air Date USA	Air Date GER	Directed by	Written by
1.10	Lebendig begraben	**Left for Dead**	Jan 6, 2004	May 26, 2005	J.Whitmore, Jr.	D.Bellisario & D.McGill

Kate immediately bonds with a woman suffering from amnesia after she wakes up and crawls from her grave following a murder attempt, claiming to remember that a bomb is present on a Navy ship and that people will die unless it's found. But unknown to Kate and the team, the anonymous Jane Doe is actually lying to Kate as she is secretly already beginning to remember who she really is and is probably planning something to strike back against her employers, something that might end in bloodshed... *Source:* [1]

Tony: Speaking of dates to work from, we've worked together for two years and, you know, I have no idea where you live.
Ducky: Well, I'd just as well we kept it that way, Tony.

Abby: I suppose you want me to tell you what chastity belt this opens?
Gibbs: Do I look like DiNozzo?
Tony: Not funny, Boss. Besides, I could open a chastity belt.
Abby: Have you ever seen one? Mine's awesome. It's eighteenth-century French.

Abby: Like when photocopiers first came out, and people were copying everything from C-notes to their butts.
Tony: You sat your naked butt on a photocopier, didn't you, Abby?
Abby: Yep.

Ducky: Jethro, I don't answer forensic questions I don't know the answers to. Why do you keep asking me?
Gibbs: *(shrugs)* Force of habit.

Tony: You remember when I stayed with you that time, when it didn't really go so well?
Gibbs: Yeah, I remember, DiNozzo.
Tony: Well, listen, I was younger then, immature, a little unfocused -
Gibbs: It was six months ago, Tony.

Tony: What is it with Germans and the alphabet thing? You know, BMW, BMG, BASF, and they're all B's.
Gibbs: I'm resisting the urge to say cut the BS.

Tony: We gotta do something, Boss.
Gibbs: Have you ever made a mistake, Tony?
Tony: According to you or to me?
Gibbs: You.
Tony: Yeah.
Gibbs: Could anyone make you feel better?
Tony: *(pause)* No.

Ducky: I don't have a body.
Gibbs: Well go find one Ducky.
Ducky: Here?
Gibbs: Sure. How many times have we had multiple victims?

Abby: Hey guys. What's you'd find?
Tony: Kate willing to give her bedroom to Jane Doe. But not me.
Abby: *(sarcastic)* Shocking.

Source: [3]

Episodes Season 1

No.	German Title	US Title	Air Date USA	Air Date GER	Directed by	Written by
1.11	Wintersonne	**Eye Spy**	Jan 13, 2004	Jun 2, 2005	A.Levi	F.Cardea, D.Coen & G.Schenck

NCIS is called in to investigate the murder of a naval officer at Little Creek Naval Base following an anonymous tip-off. McGee manages to track the tip-off to Langley, suggesting that the CIA has been spying on the base. Gibbs and Kate follow the tip-off, coming across a witness who leads the team to several possible suspects. At first the murder seems to be tied in with work the officer was involved with, but the team soon begins to suspect a more domestic motive. *Source:* [1]

Tony: I've weighed exactly the same since the day I graduated from college; never up, never down.
Kate: Certainly you would know. Do you weigh yourself a lot?
Tony: I never weigh myself.
Kate: I see.

Tony: You got me thinking, Kate; maybe I should improve my diet.
Kate: When you gonna start?
Tony: What do you call this? *(gestures with nutrition bar)*
Kate: Bad things masquerading as something good for you.

Kate: Let's see, what do we got here. High fructose corn syrup - basically, sugar. High maltose corn syrup - another sugar. Sugar! Sugar. Fractionated palm kernel oil. That sounds yummy! And contains less than two percent natural flavor. That would make it ninety-eight percent artificial flavor.
Tony: So what are you saying?

Tony: Come on, come on, McGee, you said you could do this.
McGee: But I didn't say it was gonna be easy.
Tony: Actually, that's exactly what you said, only on the phone, you ended it with a 'sir.'

Kate: With the exception of finding a decent barber, Gibbs can do pretty much anything he says he can.

Kate: You know I bet this is why number two came after you with a nine iron, isn't it? You just refused to sit down and talk things through.
Gibbs: Actually that wasn't it at all.
Kate: So what was it, then?
Gibbs: Seven iron.

Kate: We know the killer was left handed, which eliminates Commander Tyler whose service file confirms she's a rightie.
Tony: We also know the killer's a woman unless Obermaier went Norman Bates on the guy. Actually, when you think about it the MO's match. (Makes stabbing motion at Kate's back)
Gibbs: DiNozzo.
Kate: *(turns)* What'd you do?

Source: 3

Episodes Season 1

No.	German Title	US Title	Air Date USA	Air Date GER	Directed by	Written by
1.12	Ein Bein in West Virginia	**My Other Left Foot**	Feb 3, 2004	Jun 9, 2005	J.Woolnough	J.Bernstein

When the leg of a marine is discovered in a dumpster, Gibbs and the team have a problem - identifying who the leg belongs to and finding the rest of his body. Kate and Tony are ordered to find the marine's place of burial and exhume the body, only to discover that the marine to whom the leg belongs to was apparently cremated years ago. With no solid leads available, the team is stuck following red herrings, until it becomes apparent that the marine was in fact alive until recently, and another marine was killed and falsely identified in the past. This revelation prompts the NCIS team to investigate closer to home. *Source:* [1]

Tony: You really like small towns?
Kate: Peace and quiet. A place where people know you by name. No Blockbuster and Starbucks on every corner. What's not to like? Tony: Too quiet, everybody knows your name, there's no Blockbuster and Starbucks on every corner.
Kate: Big cities just can't give you what small towns can, Tony. It's a simpler way of life, a slice of Americana.
Tony: One that doesn't include fifty yard line seats to the Redskins or women with full sets of teeth.
Kate: Yeah it always comes back to that doesn't it?
Tony: See... You do get me.

Tony: I don't get the whole tattoo thing.
Kate: I'll add that to the ever-growing list of things you don't get.
Tony: Being stuck with a needle thousands of times for a piece of artwork? No thank you.
Kate: It's more than just artwork, Tony.
Tony: On a woman, maybe.
Kate: What?
Tony: You know, on a woman. Means she's up for anything.
Kate: Abby's got tattoos.
Tony: No comment.

Gibbs: Any more tattoos?
Tony: Just the rose on Kate's butt.
Gibbs: It's not a rose.

Abby: You know what they say about guys with big hands and big feet, right?
Ducky: What?
Abby: They're clowns.

Gibbs: What's wrong?
Abby: Look at it.
Gibbs: Looks like a match.
Abby: Precisely.
Gibbs: Good work, Abby.
Abby: No, it's not! You gave me 2 samples form the same tree. B matched and A didn't. I screwed up.
Gibbs: Sycamore A was from a tree down the street.
Abby: What?!
Gibbs: The idea of matching plant DNA was a bit...hinky for me.
Abby: Oh, ye of little faith!
Gibbs: Abby, c'mon! All I did was give you a blind test.
Abby: Well, you could've done that by not telling me which sample was from the suspect's sycamore!
Gibbs: I didn't think of that.

Source: [3]

Episodes Season 1

No.	German Title	US Title	Air Date USA	Air Date GER	Directed by	Written by
1.13	Todesschüsse	One Shot, One Kill	Feb 10, 2004	Jun 16, 2005	P.Ellis	G.Grant

When a marine recruiter is killed, the NCIS team quickly discover that a highly intelligent and skilled sniper was behind the attack. Initially, the team believes the sniper had a grudge against the recruiter, but when a second attack occurs the investigation takes on a wider scope. When Gibbs notices that the sniper left a calling card at each scene, he realizes that the sniper was meeting the recruiters before the shooting took place. Hoping to lure out the killer, Gibbs dons his old Marine uniform and takes over in the recruitment office with Kate, his new "commanding officer", co-ordinating with DiNozzo and assisted by an FBI team. *Source:* [1]

```
Gibbs Rule #9: Never go anywhere without a knife.

Tony: Do you think he'd let me borrow his uniform for the weekend?
Kate: I don't know. I just hope I'm there when you ask him.

Gibbs: Hey, DiNozzo, kinda reminds me of your apartment - except for that minty
fresh urine smell.
Tony: For your information, I have a maid now.
Gibbs: You can afford a maid?
Tony: It's amazing what you can do when you don't have to pay three alimonies.
(pause) Ow!

Kate: Next time drive a little faster, Tony. I think my glands have an ounce of
adrenaline left.
Tony: Response to a crime scene investigation demands a timely arrival, Kate.
Kate: It would help if the investigators didn't PUKE all over the crime scene.
Gibbs: Brings back memories.
Kate: Memories of what?
Gibbs: Marriage.
```

Source: [3]

No.	German Title	US Title	Air Date USA	Air Date GER	Directed by	Written by
1.14	Der gute Samariter	The Good Samaritan	Feb 17, 2004	Jun 23, 2005	A.Levi	J.Bernstein

A local county sheriff calls in NCIS upon discovering a murdered lieutenant commander by the roadside, quickly followed by the murder of a civilian contractor two counties over. As the team struggle to find a motive or suspects for either case, another murder occurs; this time a naval aviator. Ducky points out that while the murders appear to follow the same modus operandi and seem to have been carried out by a serial killer, some elements are different, indicating that the murders were not carried out by the same individual. A DNA sample draws suspicion onto the widow of the third victim, but she has an iron-clad alibi, leaving Gibbs with a complex investigation and many loose ends to tie up. *Source:* [1]

```
Gibbs: Anything Abby?
Abby: This is the left rear tire off Commander Julius's car. Notice anything
unusual?
Gibbs: It's inflated.
Abby: Is that a guess, or do you actually know where I'm going with this?
Gibbs: What do you think?
Abby: Well, I don't know, that's why I asked you.
Gibbs: Why don't you just tell me?
Abby: So you don't know.
Gibbs: I want to make sure you know.
Abby: Hmmmm.
Gibbs: Hmmmm.
Abby: We should play poker sometime.
Gibbs: Yeah, we should.
```

Source: [3]

Episodes Season 1

No.	German Title	US Title	Air Date USA	Air Date GER	Directed by	Written by
1.15	Der Colonel	**Enigma**	Feb 24, 2004	Jun 30, 2005	T.J.Wright	J.Kelley

Fornell and Gibbs clash when it is discovered that a marine colonel, William Ryan (Terry O'Quinn) who also happens to be Gibbs's former C.O has absconded from Iraq with two million dollars, and returned to the states under an assumed name. Fornell thinks he stole the money for himself while Gibbs denies the claim, believing he's innocent. Ryan later contacts Gibbs, and explains that he has discovered a conspiracy to siphon funds out of Iraq for use on black ops. Gibbs is drafted in to aid in bringing down the conspiracy, and meets the Colonel's partner - a lieutenant named Cameron who had actually died in Gibbs's arms years ago. After being arrested for "pissing off the FBI", Gibbs and Fornell set out to discover the truth behind the Colonel's claims in a tense standoff. It is soon discovered that Ryan is suffering from paranoid schizophrenia and after the standoff ends, he is put into a mental hospital so that he can be treated for his mental illness. *Source:* [1]

```
Gibbs Rule #12: Never date a co-worker.

Kate: Do all Marines build boats?
Tony: Only the ones who've been married a few times.
Kate: Why's that?
Tony: The rest of them can afford to buy one

Kate: So what happened?
Tony: She broke into my apartment and filled my closet with dog crap.
Kate: Ha! Really? I knew there was a reason I liked her.
Tony: I still have her number. Maybe you two can get together and boil rabbits
or something.
Kate: Not my style, Tony. I would just shoot you.
Gibbs: And that would be the reason for rule number twelve.
Kate: Rule twelve?
Gibbs: Never date a co-worker.
```
Source: [3]

No.	German Title	US Title	Air Date USA	Air Date GER	Directed by	Written by
1.16	Alptraum im Keller	**Bête Noire**	Mar 2, 2004	Jul 7, 2005	P.Ellis	D.Bellisario

Ducky responds to an emergency call when the Israeli Embassy sends a Royal Navy officer to NCIS for autopsy, only to find a gunman (revealed in later episodes to be recurring antagonist Ari Haswari) inside the body bag. As Ducky, Gerald and eventually Kate are held hostage in the autopsy lab, the director coordinates with an FBI strike team to negotiate their release. Meanwhile, Kate hesitates when presented with an opportunity to kill her captor, while Gibbs and Tony take more pro-active measures to get their co-workers out safely, ending with a showdown during which shots are fired, one of which hits Gibbs's left shoulder, leaving both himself and Gerald who had been shot during the siege injured. *Source:* [1]

```
Ari: Same way I came in?
Kate: I don't know how you came in.
Ari: In a body bag.
Kate: Same way you're going out!

Gibbs: He**. I still use a notebook and a pencil, instead of a PDQ.
Tony: It's a PDA. You can call it a Palm Pilot.
Gibbs: It desn't matter what I call it if i can't use it!
Tony: I'll teach you.
Gibbs: You'll teach me? McGee teaches you! You teach me! It's backwards! I need
coffee.
```
Source: [3]

Episodes Season 1

No.	German Title	US Title	Air Date USA	Air Date GER	Directed by	Written by
1.17	Fünf Musketiere	**The Truth is Out There**	Mar 16, 2004	Jul 14, 2005	D.Smith	J.Bernstein

During a rave party, the body of a Petty Officer falls through the ceiling. Preliminary investigation suggests that the Petty Officer was killed in the nearby parking lot, and was dressed after his death. Upon checking the victim's room, evidence surfaces that he may have been taking financial bribes. Gibbs suspects the victim's co-workers of involvement in the death when their separate versions of events are too consistent. Forensic evidence links them to the scene, and they eventually confess that the death was a prank gone wrong, but Gibbs still believes that there's more to the case than meets the eye. *Source: 1*

```
Abby: Do you have any fetishes?
Gibbs: I have three ex-wives. I can't afford any fetishes.

Tony: Have you ever been in a men's room before?
Kate: No. Have you?

Kate: Never put anything on videotape that you don't want to be seen.
Tony: Just ask Paris Hilton.
```

Source: 3

No.	German Title	US Title	Air Date USA	Air Date GER	Directed by	Written by
1.18	Falsche Fährten	**UnSEALed**	Apr 6, 2004	Jul 21, 2005	P.Ellis	T.Moran

A former Navy SEAL convicted of double homicide escapes from Leavenworth, resulting in Kate and McGee being assigned to protect the son and in-laws of the escaped prisoner. During the night, the SEAL breaks into the house to see his son before fleeing, leaving Todd tied to a chair and unarmed, her weapon having been taken by the SEAL. Profiling his behavior, Kate theorizes that he may actually be innocent, and had discovered the identity of the real killer while in jail. Gibbs brings in the presiding defense and prosecution attorneys, one of which is Lt. Commander Faith Coleman to go over the evidence while attempting to arrest the true killer before the fugitive finds the actual murderer and delivers his own brand of justice: revenge. *Source: 1*

```
Tony: She sleeps with a gun boss...
Gibbs: Is that true?
Kate: Sort of...sometimes..yes
Gibbs (grins): Good Girl

Tony: Do we know what this guy was in for?
Gibbs: Same thing I'm gonna be if you don't get your a** moving.
Tony: Right. (whispering to Kate) Murder.
Kate: And you didn't even use a lifeline.

Kate: For the sake of argument, lets say he's innocent.
Tony: Why?
Gibbs: Because I said so.
Tony: Inocent, sure, why not.

Gibbs: Are you thinkin' what I think you're thinkin'?
Tony: I don't know, Boss.Are you thinkin' what I think you're thinkin'?
```

Source: 3

Episodes Season 1

No.	German Title	US Title	Air Date USA	Air Date GER	Directed by	Written by
1.19	Wenn Tote sprechen	**Dead Man Talking**	Apr 27, 2004	Jul 28, 2005	D.Smith	F.Cardea & G.Schenck

Special Agent Chris Pacci is brutally murdered while investigating a cold case, prompting a guilt-ridden Gibbs to step in and take over the case while attempting to find Pacci's killer. The team follows the trail of millions of dollars, and is led to a woman with ties to the thief. The agents take shifts conducting a stake-out on the woman's house, until Tony's caught raiding the mailbox. Forced to improvise, he introduces himself as a resident of the neighbourhood and strikes up a conversation based on what he had heard via surveillance. This gives him a chance to get close to the suspect in order to find out more, as he goes on a successful date with her. Meanwhile, Abby makes a shocking discovery which leaves Tony horrified and vulnerable to an onslaught of merciless taunts and teasing from Kate: the suspect they've been trailing, Amanda Reed is in fact Lt. Commander Voss, the Officer who faked his own death in a car accident and who's responsible for stealing money from the Navy. Things come to a head in a bar where Voss/Reed attempts to kill Tony in front of witnesses but Gibbs gets there just in time and shoots Voss/Reed dead, avenging Pacci's death. *Source:* [1]

Abby: Reminds me of the Crying Game.
McGee: Don't know it.
Abby: It was such a cool flick.
Tony: Abby, could you pick some other movie please.
Abby: Oh um Victor Victoria?
Tony: That was a girl pretending to be a guy pretending to be a girl?
Abby: Right.
Tony: Yeah. That one's ok.

Abby: You rule
Gibbs: I know...but remind me why?

Abby To McGee: Whatever you do, do not lie. Gibbs is like Santa Claus, he knows if you've been naughty.

Gibbs: Problem?
Kate: Well, you really want to do that to McGee? Special Agent Bligh...*(gesturing to Tony)*...here is going to eat him alive.
Tony: McGee looks up to me, as a mentor.
Kate: Ugh.
Gibbs: You want to be stuck in a cramped apartment with DiNozzo? Be my guest.
Kate: On the other hand, it'll help McGee build character.

Kate: I'm warning you DiNozzo, don't even go there.
(Kate leaves)
Tony: We've gotta go there. Any ideas, McGee?
McGee: No.
Tony: Well, don't worry. I've got plenty.
McGee: You realize that any prank we play on Kate we'll also be pulling on Gibbs?
Tony: That's a problem.
McGee: Unless...nah.
Tony: What?
McGee: Well, I was thinking. Since she is expecting something, maybe we should do nothing.
Tony: ...That's brilliant. It'll drive her nuts trying to figure out what we did, that we didn't do. You're all right McGee.

Gibbs: *(to Tony about information)* Are you going to spit it out, or do I have to waste my coffee on your head?

Source: [3]

Episodes Season 1

No.	German Title	US Title	Air Date USA	Air Date GER	Directed by	Written by
1.20	Willkommen in der Hölle	**Missing**	May 4, 2004	Aug 4, 2005	J.Woolnough	J.Kelley

The disappearance of a marine draws NCIS in to investigate, and it's discovered that several marines from the same unit have also vanished under similar circumstances. When skeletal remains of one of the missing men is found chained to a pipe in a small sewer room, Gibbs begins to suspect the unit CO (the only team member not dead or missing) as a serial killer. However, after Tony vanishes, the investigation takes on a more frantic pace and McGee is called in from Norfolk to help as Gibbs and Kate work against the clock to find Tony before it's too late. *Source: 1*

Gibbs Rule #9: Never go anywhere without a knife.

Tony: Admit it, you were worried about me. *(no response)* You don't have to say it. I know. *(still no response)* Okay, I want you to say it. You do care right? *(elevator doors open and Gibbs walks out)* So.....are you saying you don't care?
Gibbs: *(stops)* Tony, as far as I'm concerned *(taps his cheeks)*, you're irreplaceable.
Tony: I knew it *(laughs a little)*. I knew behind the whole marine thing you really are at heart--
Gibbs: Forget it McGee he's still alive.

Kate: Tony, you are so lucky you didn't have sisters growing up.
Tony: Why's that?
Kate: Because youd never have reached puberty. Of course, one could argue you still haven't reached it.

Kate: You were pretty tough with her.
Gibbs: She reminds me of my ex-wife.
Tony: Which one?
Gibbs: All of them!

Source: 3

No.	German Title	US Title	Air Date USA	Air Date GER	Directed by	Written by
1.21	Verbotene Waffen	**Split Decision**	May 11, 2004	Aug 11, 2005	T.O'Hara	B.Gookin

As Ducky meets his new assistant, Jimmy Palmer, Gibbs takes the case of a marine found impaled on a tree stump. The investigation uncovers the sale of decommissioned military weapons on the black market. Tony goes undercover and meets the buyer, only to stumble into an ATF operation. Working with ATF Special Agent Stone, Gibbs poses as a weapons supplier to complete the deal, and must double cross everyone in order to find the corrupt person at the centre of the investigation, and the one responsible for the marine's death. *Source: 1*

Gibbs: Abs, leave a few gaps, don't make it so neat.
Abby: Please Gibbs, I've been making fake IDs since I was 15.

Abby: It's not like they have any new ideas. It's just so...
Ducky: The song remains the same?
Abby: Exactly. And bonus points for the gratuitous rock reference.

Tony: He said you could use his computer?
McGee: Uh huh.
Tony: Really? You know, when mine fried, he wouldn't let me touch his.
Gibbs: 'Cause your fingers are always greasy from fried chicken and pizza.

Source: 3

Episodes Season 1

No.	German Title	US Title	Air Date USA	Air Date GER	Directed by	Written by
1.22	Abgestürzt	**A Weak Link**	May 18,2004	Aug 18, 2005	A.Levi	J.Bernstein

Routine training results in the death of a U.S. Navy SEAL lieutenant just days before he was due to deploy on a classified hostage rescue operation. The death is initially dismissed as an equipment malfunction, but Abby discovers that the link attaching the lieutenant to his rappelling rope was made of a weaker material than factory standard, suggesting sabotage and potentially murder. Pressure is applied by the CIA for the investigation to be wrapped up within 38 hours so the operation can continue or else the entire mission will be scrubbed. As the case goes on, Gibbs discovers that the lieutenant had a secret, and that his wife might be holding back vital information about his death. *Source:* [1]

Gibbs: Let's pretend we don't know anything.
Tony: Not much of a stretch.

Gibbs: What if I wanted to get into that account?
Kate: Get a search warrent for the servers.
Gibbs: Don't have time for a warrent. What's a quicker way?
Kate: Hack in the server.
(Gibbs smiles)
Kate: I can't believe I just said that.I would have never suggested that before I started working here.
Gibbs: You're welcome.

Gibbs: DiNozzo, was there something in my tone of voice that made that sound like a suggestion? *Source:* [3]

No.	German Title	US Title	Air Date USA	Air Date GER	Directed by	Written by
1.23	Der Terrorist	**Reveille**	May 25, 2004	Aug 25, 2005	T.J.Wright	D.Bellisario

As Gibbs's obsession with tracking down the infiltrator who held Todd and Ducky hostage begins reaching new heights, the team grow more concerned about him. McGee works at identifying him with a modified FBI program, while Todd and Tony go for lunch with Ducky. As Tony leaves in pursuit of his "dream woman" who is actually a terrorist, Kate heads back to the office for a video conference with Paula Cassidy, only to be kidnapped and reunited with her captor, now revealed as a Hamas terrorist who is planning to shoot down Marine One - a transport helicopter carrying President Bush and Ariel Sharon. At first, she refuses to cooperate, but she reluctantly relents when the female terrorist threatens to kill Tony after sleeping with him. As Gibbs grows increasingly agitated, the search for the terrorist is narrowed down by McGee and Abby calculating his exact age, and Ducky concluding that he attended medical school. McGee's program locates him as a graduate of a Scottish medical school. As the terrorist tries to convince Kate to identify Marine One, McGee finally discovers his name - Ari Haswari. It is soon revealed that Marine One cannot be identified out of the other choppers and that Haswari is actually an undercover Mossad operative in Al-Qaeda. He infiltrated the Hamas cell to draw them into a trap, making them believe that Marine One could be identified. ... *Source:* [1]

Gibbs: Rule No.7: Always be specific when you lie.

Gibbs: He stay at your place?
Abby: Yep.
Gibbs: You sleep in the coffin, McGee? McGee: *(looks at Abby)* Coffin?
Well...you...you said it was a box sofa bed.
Abby: Well...it is...sort of.
McGee: That's why you wouldn't turn the lights on! *(scoffs)* I can't believe I slept in a coffin.
Abby: *(shrugs)* Not just slept. *Source:* [3]

Season 2 (Episodes 2.24- 2.46)

Originally broadcast between September 28, 2004 and May 24, 2005, the second season shifts away from the naval setting of the show somewhat, and includes more character development than the first season. Season 2 saw Norfolk Case Agent Timothy McGee being promoted to a full-time field agent, and transferring to NCIS HQ in Washington to work with the Major Case Response Team. Tony DiNozzo nearly died of the pneumonic plague in "SWAK" while in the season finale, "Twilight," Caitlin Todd was shot and killed by Ari Haswari.

Source: [1]

Original Air Date USA	September 28, 2004 – May 24, 2005 on CBS
Original Air Date German Language	September 1, 2005 – March 9, 2006 on Sat 1

Episodes Season 2

No.	German Title	US Title	Air Date USA	Air Date GER	Directed by	Written by
2.24	Unsichtbar	**See No Evil**	Sep 28, 2004	Sep 1, 2005	T.Wright	C.Crowe

When an eight-year-old blind girl Sandy Watson (played by Abigail Breslin) and her mother, Jill are kidnapped to blackmail a Navy captain (David Keith) into transferring $2 million in government funds, Gibbs and his team are faced with a unique challenge. An unexpected twist is uncovered when Abby and McGee manage to trace the money. The twist is that Captain Watson is the one responsible for arranging the kidnapping in the first place as he wanted to steal money from the government. After helping them solve the case, Tim McGee who was on a brief transfer from Norfolk gets an unexpected surprise from Gibbs: he is promoted to a full-time field agent and as a result is transferred to the Navy Yard, becoming a permanent member of Gibbs's team in the process. *Source:* [1]

```
Kate:  "When I'm a mother, I'm never letting my kids out of my sight."
Tony:  "Yeah, how do you plan on doing that? "
Kate:  "G-P-S locater strapped to the ankle. Audio and video surveillance built
into their clothes."
Tony:  "No, I mean the part about becoming a mother."

Kate: Can't you tell when somebody's kidding with you, McGee?
McGee: I used to and then I met you guys.

Gibbs: McGee, where are you going?
McGee: Uh, Norfolk.
Gibbs: Well, I got some good news and some bad news.You've just been promoted
to a full time field agent.
McGee: Really? That's incredible! What's...
Gibbs: You belong to me now!

Abby: Face it, McGee. We are doomed.
McGee: Gibbs can't really expect us to hack into the pentagon in a single
afternoon!
Abby: Yeah, he can.
McGee: You're right, we are doomed.
```

Source: [3]

Episodes Season 2

No.	German Title	US Title	Air Date USA	Air Date GER	Directed by	Written by
2.25	Die perfekte Frau	**The Good Wives Club**	Oct 5, 2004	Sep 8, 2005	D.Smith	G.Grant

The mummified remains of a woman wearing a single wedding dress are found in an abandoned Marine home. The fact that the room the victim was in was modelled on the 1950s leads the team to suspect that a serial killer, one who endured horrific abuse as a child is responsible for the crime. And in the search for answers, McGee uncovers a missing person's report, this one in Jacksonville regarding a Petty Officer who had vanished on her way to work months and who has been missing for four months. The team then head to the Base and begin working with the NCIS Special Agent there in the hope of finding the missing Officer before it's too late and to also stop the killer once and for all. *Source:* [1]

Gibbs: "What do you have Abby?"
Abby: "What don't I have Gibbs? Clothing fibers, carpet fibers, dust, beetle parts, soiled bedding, there's even a pamphlet called "The Good Wives Guide" what's up with that?"
Gibbs: "Ask McGee."
Abby: "McGee?"
Gibbs: "Ma-Gee"
Abby: "Really?"

Gibbs: Put someone in a wedding dress.
Kate: Tony would look cute.
Gibbs: No. He's off interviewing the victim's parents.
Kate: Well, McGee then.
Gibbs: No, he's with Tony.
Kate: Abby.
Gibbs: No, up to her tatts in forensic tests.
Kate: Well, what about you? (Gibbs gives her a look) You won't have to wear the dress.
Tony: *[at weird crime scene]* This is really sick. Stephen King would love it.

Source: [3]

No.	German Title	US Title	Air Date USA	Air Date GER	Directed by	Written by
2.26	Auge um Auge	**Vanished**	Oct 12, 2004	Sep 15, 2005	T.Wright	C.Crowe

A marine attack helicopter is discovered in the middle of a crop circle in a rural area and both the pilots who were originally thought to have been on aboard, are missing. Soon, NCIS discovers that only one of the pilots was on the flight and that there is a ten year feud going on in the town of Smokey Corners, West Virginia andas a result, the missing pilot on the run, seeking revenge for something while some of the locals are going to great lengths to hide secrets that could help solve the case. *Source:* [1]

Ducky: "DNA doesn't lie, Jethro. People do"

Kate: "Most people tend to their personal hygiene at home."
Tony: "This bothers you?"
Kate: "No, what bothers me is that it doesn't bother me anymore."
Tony: "I'm an acquired taste."
McGee: "Actually, it's more like the Stockholm Syndrome. The emotional attachment to a captor formed by a hostage as a result of continuous stress and a need to cooperate for survival."
[after telling McGee about a movie which depict the parents as aliens]
Tony: Whew! Scared of my parents for years after that.
McGee: I'm sure the feeling was mutual.

Source: [3]

Episodes Season 2

No.	German Title	US Title	Air Date USA	Air Date GER	Directed by	Written by
2.27	Neptuns Zeichen	**Lt. Jane Doe**	Oct 19, 2004	Sep 22, 2005	D.Smith	G.Grant

While on leave, two sailors discover the body of a young woman dressed in a Navy uniform and due to the fact that she has no ID on her is given the name, Lt. Jane Doe. However, the case becomes very personal for Ducky when he realizes that it bears a striking resemblance to a similar case that he investigated ten years ago... *Source:* [1]

```
Jimmy: Ducky went to Norfolk. I think he drove.
Gibbs: Why?
Jimmy: Why did he drive?
Gibbs: No, why did he go to Norfolk!!!
Ducky: Unlike the living, when the dead speak, they do not lie.

McGee: If I said that to Gibbs, I would be seeing stars.
Abby: Well that's the advantage of being me.

Tony: Do you believe in Karma Boss?
Gibbs: I've had three wives, DiNozzo.
```

Source: [3]

No.	German Title	US Title	Air Date USA	Air Date GER	Directed by	Written by
2.28	Der Maulwurf	**The Bone Yard**	Oct 26, 2004	Sep 29, 2005	T.O'Hara	J.C.Kelley

The NCIS team attends a crime scene, and end up finding multiple remains among the wreckage. When one set of remains is revealed to be an undercover FBI agent, the team realises that they've stumbled upon a dumping ground which the mob have been using for eighteen years to dispose of their victims. The FBI suspect an agency mole is responsible for the exposure and subsequent death of the murdered agent, and it appears as though Fornell's being set up to take the blame for what's going on. Gibbs then sets out to find the real mole and clear Fornell's name, using tactics that shock his team. *Source:* [1]

```
Kate: "Maybe we don't need one. That is, if you're ready to become a father"
Tony: "I think she's talking to you, Probie"
Kate: "We go down to the lab and see if I'm carrying your baby. It'll be fun"
McGee: "Oh! And we can steal Little Rickey's DNA test"
Kate: "Photograph it for Abby"
Tony: "I'll do it"
McGee: "Why you?"
Tony: "Do you think anyone would believe you actually slept with Kate?"

Kate:" Wow, I thought you were the only one who could piss him off like that."
Tony: "You never met his second wife."

Abby: Hear Kate kicked your butt this morning, McGee.
McGee: Oh. You heard wrong. Wasn't my butt...
Abby: So she kicked you in the...?
McGee: I thought I was joining a Federal Agency, not reliving my junior year in high school.
Abby: Just remember, they torture you because they care.
McGee: So, if I make them dislike me...?
Abby: It'll get worse.
```

Source: [3]

Episodes Season 2

No.	German Title	US Title	Air Date USA	Air Date GER	Directed by	Written by
2.29	Schatten der Angst	**Terminal Leave**	Nov 16, 2004	Oct 6, 2005	R.Director	J.Woolnough

When an Iraq veteran is threatened and very nearly killed by a group of terrorists, the NCIS team steps in to protect her and her family from further danger. While trying to convince an FBI agent to help them, the team is convinced that they've discovered the bomber. However, things might not be what they seem when another car bomb nearly kills Tony and Kate during their protection duty of the Lieutenant Commander. In the meantime, a single family secret may pose more of a threat than even terrorists could. *Source:* [1]

Kate: "Tony."
Tony: "Yes, Kate dear."
Kate: "There's only one bathroom downstairs."
Tony: "And your point is?"
Kate: "The seat stays down."
Tony: "Unless it's up."

Kate: *(from the shower)* Tony! Out of here. Now!
Tony: What? I'm just brushing my teeth. Oh, hey, don't use up the hot water 'cause you've been in there forever.
Kate: Tony, how long have you been in here?
Tony: Long enough to know you can't sing... and haven't shaved your legs in a week.

Tony: Oh, sounds like we're goin' to need the infrared scope on this one, McGee.
McGee: The one that can see through walls at night?
Tony: Better than pay-TV. And the best part? It's free.
Kate: And that's the reason why, Tony.
Tony: Why what, Kate?
Kate: You'll never get my home address.

Source: [3]

No.	German Title	US Title	Air Date USA	Air Date GER	Directed by	Written by
2.30	Der Held von Iwo Jima	**Call of Silence**	Nov 23, 2004	13. Oct 13, 2005	T.Wright	R.Director

A former Marine, and Medal of Honor recipient who fought In World War II (played by Charles Durning), confesses to having murdered his friend in battle. Gibbs does not believe this is the whole truth and goes on to prove his innocence. The team become personally involved with the case, with Gibbs using deceptive tactics to pull the truth from the elderly man. *Source:* [1]

Kate: Coleman is going to use this to put Yost away for the rest of his life.
Tony: Do we have to tell her?
Gibbs: *(sarcastically)* No. Here at NCIS we just report the evidence we like.

Henry: "Gibbs."
Gibbs: "Hey, Morning Henry."
Henry: "That sushi place you sent me to,"
Gibbs: "What, you didn't like it?"
Henry: "I liked it fine. Only, you didn't tell me I had to speak Japaneses to order."
Gibbs: "You don't order, you eat what you're served with a smile. Just like being married."

Source: [3]

Episodes Season 2

No.	German Title	US Title	Air Date USA	Air Date GER	Directed by	Written by
2.31	Herzenssachen	**Heart Break**	Nov 30, 2004	Oct 20, 2005	D.Smith	G.Schenck & F.Cardea

A Navy Commander dies after a successful surgery. At first glance, it appears that the sudden death might have been a case of spontaneous human combustion. While researching the dead man's past, the team discovers that he had gained a lot of enemies recently, not least of all a young ensign, who makes himself the prime suspect with some bizarre behaviour. However, while analysing the evidence from the scene of the death, Abby and Tony discover the truth, and in turn find a new suspect. In the meantime, Ducky develops a soft spot for the doctor who was treating the commander. *Source:* [1]

```
Tony: I saw that movie!
Ducky: The silent version, or the British mini series?
Tony: They were talking.

Tony: Too bad you didn't get to bed at a sensible hour. I mean, to sleep, cause
obviously, you were in bed.
Kate: I get it, Tony.
```
Source: [3]

No.	German Title	US Title	Air Date USA	Air Date GER	Directed by	Written by
2.32	Leere Augen	**Forced Entry**	Dec 7, 2004	Oct 27, 2005	D.Smith	J.Stern & J.C.Kelley

A Marine's wife shoots an intruder in self defense when he is about to rape her but things change when Gibbs and the team uncoverevidence suggesting that she might have lured her supposed attacker to her home under the guise of a date. *Source:* [1]

```
Gibbs Rule #23: Never mess with a Marine's coffee if you want to live.

Gibbs: Hey Kate, your brothers are really like that?
Kate: Sadly, yes.
Gibbs: Huh, explains a lot.

McGee: Well, there's about a 150 gigabytes of data on several hard drives.
Gibbs: Only a 150?
(Gibbs pat McGee on the shoulder)
Gibbs: Hell, that shouldn't take much time at all.
McGee: He has no idea what a gigabyte is, does he Abby?
Abby: I don't think he knows what a hard drive is McGee.
```
Source: [3]

No.	German Title	US Title	Air Date USA	Air Date GER	Directed by	Written by
2.33	Flucht in Ketten	**Chained**	Dec 14, 2004	Nov 3, 2005	T.Wright	F.Military

Tony goes undercover as an escaped prisoner. He is tasked with sticking to a convict who has information about stolen Iraqi antiques. During the investigation, Tony disappears, and the GPS locator that Abby placed on him is no longer working. After some startling discoveries in the case including information that the convict Tony is accompanying may in fact be a murderer with blood on his hands, the team realise that Tony's life may be in danger and race against time to find him before it's too late. *Source:* [1]

```
Kate: EEEK!
(over the monitor)
Abby: What's wrong?
Kate: Gibbs is driving.
Abby: I'm saying a prayer in many languages.
```
Source: [3]

Episodes Season 2

No.	German Title	US Title	Air Date USA	Air Date GER	Directed by	Written by
2.34	Ein Mann für unlösbare Fälle	**Black Water**	Jan 11, 2005	Nov 10, 2005	T.O'Hara	J.C.Coto & J.C.Kelley

A Navy officer's body is found in a car pulled from a lake by a celebrity private investigator. The man had been missing for two years. The PI now wants to claim the reward posted by the family, but the NCIS team must complete the investigation to find the killer before the money is awarded. The case changes from accidental death to suspected murder when McGee discovers a bullet lodged in the car. The team initially suspect that the dead man's brother may be a prime suspect, but forensic evidence suggests someone unexpected is responsible for the killing. *Source:* [1]

Ducky: Do you suspect foul play?
Gibbs: Oh, you know me, Duck... I suspect everything.
Ducky: Yes, an admirable trait in an investigator. And also the reason your three marriages ended in divorce.
Gibbs: Oh yeah? All these years I thought it was because I was a b*****.

Jimmy: Did you ever meet any of special agent Gibbs' wives?
Ducky: Actually, I presented him to the last one.
Jimmy: What went wrong?
Ducky: I don't know, she doesn't speak to me anymore.

McGee: I'm not surprised you haven't heard of it. There's no pictures in it.
Tony: Did you say something, Probie?
McGee: Yeah. I'm not a dork."
Tony: Whatever you say, Sponge Bob.

Source: [3]

No.	German Title	US Title	Air Date USA	Air Date GER	Directed by	Written by
2.35	Doppeltes Spiel	**Doppelgänger**	Jan 18, 2005	Nov 17, 2005	T.O'Hara	D.Bellisario & J.Bernstein

A telemarketer hears a murder while trying to sell a long distance call package. The team investigates with the help of a civilian law enforcement team whose personalities seem to be an exact copy of Gibbs and his team. Each team member discovers different crucial facts about the case, leading to the discovery that the murder may not have been all it seemed to be. When Abby and McGee discover that the dead man was using the Navy computer system for his own financial gain, they consult with the people he worked with to see if they can shed light on who may have wanted him dead. But the investigation becomes more intense when the missing Petty Officer is actually found dead and the team find themselves hunting down his killer. *Source:* [1]

McGee: Where are we going, Boss?
Gibbs: To talk to Petty Officer Lambert's shipmates.
McGee: He's not on a ship, Boss. Oh, sorry. You were using a military euphemism.
Gibbs: You think?
McGee: So you mean Bethesda Hospital Computer Center.
Gibbs: You speak their language.
McGee: You mean I'm going to interview them?
Gibbs: I interview, you translate. Come on!

Abby: No one gets everything right the first time, McGee. Except Gibbs.

Source: [3]

Episodes Season 2

No.	German Title	US Title	Air Date USA	Air Date GER	Directed by	Written by
2.36	Blutiges Puzzle	**The Meat Puzzle**	Feb 8, 2005	Nov 24, 2005	F.Wright	F.Military

After several months, Ducky and Jimmy finally start identifying the bodies in the meat puzzle they have been working on. It is not long before Ducky realises he testified in the court case of a would-be Medical Examiner named Vincent Hanlon who was accused of murder and was eventually jailed for eight years as a result. They soon discover that the dead men were involved in the case and it dawns on Gibbs that Ducky might be the next target. Tony and Kate are assigned to protection detail which means safeguarding Ducky and his elderly mother, but a mistake by Kate leads to Ducky being kidnapped from his home during the night. The team must race against time to find him before he ends up dead like all the other previous victims while Jimmy and Abby begin working together to uncover the truth. *Source:* [1]

Kate: Gibbs, what did Ducky look like when he was younger?
Gibbs: Illya Kuryakin.

Abby: I am one of the few people in the world who can murder you and leave no forensic evidence.

Source: [3]

No.	German Title	US Title	Air Date USA	Air Date GER	Directed by	Written by
2.37	Die Zeugin	**Witness**	Feb 15, 2005	Dec 1, 2005	J.Whitmore jr.	G.Schenck & F.Cardea

A beautiful young MIT graduate (Danica McKellar) witnesses a sailor being strangled. Local police doubt her story, but McGee asserts that her account warrants further investigation. When a sailor's body is found at another location, the story gains ground. The witness also captivates McGee who, after a sudden twist in the investigation, ends up unknowingly holding the key to solving the case. *Source:* [1]

McGee: What do you got, Abs?
Abby: *(to Gibbs)* Do I have to answer the newbie?
Gibbs: Humor him.

Gibbs: Any more food fights in here and I'm joining in. With peas.
Kate: Frozen peas?
Gibbs: Nope. In a can.

Source: [3]

No.	German Title	US Title	Air Date USA	Air Date GER	Directed by	Written by
2.38	Männer und Frauen	**Caught on Tape**	Feb 22, 2005	Dec 8, 2005	J.Woolnough	C.Crowe, G.Grant, J.C.Kelley

A Marine falls off a cliff, and his camera records him falling to his death. The prime suspects are his wife and his best friend with whom he was staying in the camp. Gibbs finds out they had an affair behind a dead man's back and he tries to persuade them to blame each other. In the meantime, Abby reconstructs the damaged film footage on the camera and reveals a previously dismissed suspect to have been in the vicinity at the time of death *Source:* [1]

Gibbs: What do you think?
Kate: The word disgusting comes to mind.
Gibbs: Do you smell that?
Kate: If you mean the urine's, then YEH.

Source: [3]

Episodes Season 2

No.	German Title	US Title	Air Date USA	Air Date GER	Directed by	Written by
2.39	Wege zum Ruhm	**Pop Life**	Mar 1, 2005	Dec 15, 2005	T.Wright	F.Military

A dance club bartender wakes up in bed with a dead female petty officer and claims this was not the woman he came home with, despite the fact that he was drunk at the time. DNA tests reveal that he was telling the truth, but the team must still work to figure out whether this means that he didn't kill the dead woman. The victim's sister and a local corrupt businessman may know more than they are telling. Guest Starring Mya. *Source:* [1]

```
Tony: I knew this girl once. She squeaked. She made this little squeaking...
Kate: Tony! You want to tell Ducky that story?
Gibbs: He's heard it. We all have.

Gibbs: Are you done?
Tony: Almost.
Gibbs: Done or fired. Those are your options.
Tony: Done.
```
Source: [3]

No.	German Title	US Title	Air Date USA	Air Date GER	Directed by	Written by
2.40	Blau wie Kobalt	**An Eye for an Eye**	Mar 22, 2005	Jan 12, 2006	D.Smith	S.Kano

When a Petty Officer working in Intelligence receives a pair of cobalt blue eyeballs in the mail, the NCIS team starts investigating the case. The sailor commits suicide during the investigation and after Abby matches the eyes to a South American girl in a photo with the dead man's lecturer, Kate and Tony must travel to the Triple Frontier destination of Paraguay to discover the truth.. *Source:* [1]

```
McGee: Hey, you know what this reminds me of? Pacci's suspect that we were
staking out last year.
Kate: That's right! The beautiful pre-op transsexual who seduced Tony.
Tony: She didn't seduce me. I was undercover.
Kate: Yeah, well didn't you stick your tongue down...
Tony: I took one for the team, all right? Someone had to keep her occupied.
McGee: Don't you mean him?
```
Source: [3]

No.	German Title	US Title	Air Date USA	Air Date GER	Directed by	Written by
2.41	Bikini Girl	**Bikini Wax**	Mar 29, 2005	Jan 19, 2006	S.Cragg	D.North

A Virginia Beach bikini contestant drowns in a public bathroom toilet. When the team discover she posed partially naked in a magazine, and was pregnant at the time of her death, clues are revealed that lead to an unlikely suspect. Tony finds a juicy secret from Kate's past. *Source:* [1]

```
Kate: "Gibbs would never walk in here and tells us how much he paid for his
shirt."
Tony: "That's because the prices have been pretty consistent at Sears since the
late seventy's."

Kate: "Give it five seconds."
McGee: "Until what?"
Kate: "Until he notices there's a..."
Tony : "Bikini contest!"
```
Source: [3]

Episodes Season 2

No.	German Title	US Title	Air Date USA	Air Date GER	Directed by	Written by
2.42	Stimmen	**Conspiracy Theory**	Apr 12, 2005	Jan 26, 2006	F.Military	J.Woolnough

The team investigates a suicide case, believing that the main reason of her death is a nervous breakdown, but Ducky believes that she was actually murdered. FBI Special Agent Fornell helps them in the investigation. The team discovers that the dead woman was involved in a love triangle and that this may have contributed to her death. *Source:* [1]

```
Abby: It's complicated.
Gibbs: You don't know do you?
Abby: Not a clue.
```

Source:

No.	German Title	US Title	Air Date USA	Air Date GER	Directed by	Written by
2.43	Die rote Zelle	**Red Cell**	Apr 26, 2005	Feb 2, 2006	D.Smith	C.Silber

A marine is found dead on the school campus, his neck broken and the team immediately finds a suspect. However, they are forced to start again when they find the suspect has also suffered the same fate as the victim, having had his neck broken with his body being buried in a construction site. McGee and Abby discover a trace in the e-mails, a mysterious group called "Red Cell," which leads the team to believe that the marine must have been involved in a serious death game. *Source:* [1]

```
Kate: "I hate to say it but that was actually smart, Tony"
Gibbs:" What was, Kate?"
Kate: "Tony might have figured out how to find the hacker"
Gibbs:" It's his job. You think I keep him around for his personality?"

Kate: "The place needs a lot of work McGee."
Tony: "At least you're not building a boat in your basement."
```

Source: [3]

No.	German Title	US Title	Air Date USA	Air Date GER	Directed by	Written by
2.44	Mit allen Ehren	**Hometown Hero**	May, 3 2005	Feb 9, 2006	J.Whitmore jr.	G.Schneck & F.Cardea

The executor of a petty officer's will discovers the skeletal remains of a missing girl in the dead man's rented storage unit. As the petty officer who died in Iraq is up for a Silver Star, it is very important that NCIS determines if he was a murderer within 24 hours or else the Silver Star will be cancelled altogether. Soil samples and further forensics lead Abby to discover that if the Marine was the killer, he could not have acted alone. Tony and McGee find CCTV footage that suggests the Marine was entirely innocent. Tony also has to deal with his car being stolen. *Source:* [1]

```
Kate: "Tony's car was towed. Poor baby had to take the bus to work"
Tony: "You know what kind of people take the bus?"
McGee: "Yeah, I take the bus"
Tony: "Exactly!"
Tony: "Do you realize Mother Teresa would have road rage hell out there?"
McGee:" I know it's a long shot"
Tony: "A long shot is you getting laid by Penelope Cruz, McGee!"
```

Source: [3]

Episodes Season 2

No.	German Title	US Title	Air Date USA	Air Date GER	Directed by	Written by
2.45	Todeskuss	**SWAK**	May 10, 2005	Mar 2, 2006	D.Smith	D.Bellisario

All hell breaks loose at the NCIS office when Tony opens a mysterious letter containing a small puff of white powder which may be a deadly bacteria. Kate calls for help and as a precaution, she and Tony are put into a bio-hazard isolation room while McGee and Gibbs are left to discover who sent the envelope and their reasons for doing so while searching for a cure to help their friends before it's too late *Source:* [1]

Gibbs: "Kate, play it safe. Go with Tony."
Kate: "That's safe?!!!"

Tony: If I get Anthrax how would you feel?
Gibbs: Not as bad as you DiNozzo.

Tony: "I have allergies"
Gibbs: "Never had allergies. Never had a cold either."
Kate: "You don't get colds?"
Gibbs: "Nope. Never had the flu either."
Kate: *(whispers to DiNozzo)* "Why do I believe him?"
Tony: "If you were a bug, would you attack Gibbs?"
McGee: "(I)Get colds all the time."
Tony: " 'Course you do, Probie."

McGee: "Wish I had my PDA."
Gibbs: "Use Ducky's."
Palmer: "Ah... Agent Gibbs, sir...Dr. Mallard doesn't have...."
Gibbs: "Requisition replacement cell phones and weapons for my team. Go!"
Palmer: "Pistols?"
Gibbs: "Well, no, Palmer, crossbows, if you think they might work better."
McGee: "Boss, I can't find Ducky's PDA."
Gibbs: "McGee, it's a pad and a pencil."

Abby: "You got to get a life, Gibbs."
Gibbs: "Last thing I need is another wife."
Abby: "Life. You got to get a life."

Gibbs: "I thought these tests were fast."
Abby: "It's not a pregnancy test."

Ducky: "Where do you think you're going?"
Gibbs: "Find out who sent the letter."
Ducky: "You cannot leave autopsy! It's negative-pressured so airborne pathogens can't contaminate the the building."
Gibbs: "I've been scrubbed, sanitized for all I know, sterilized. I have an investigation to open."
Ducky: "I have a possible contagion to contain. Until your blood test clears you, I cannot permit you to leave this room."

Source: [3]

Episodes Season 2

No.	German Title	US Title	Air Date USA	Air Date GER	Directed by	Written by
2.46	Die Rückkehr	**Twilight**	May 24, 2005	Mar 9, 2006	T.Wright	J.C.Kelley

With Ari Haswari back in the country again and out to kill Gibbs, the team find themselves attempting to stop Ari from completing the task. In the meantime, they also try to find out who killed two off-duty sailors whose deaths might be linked to an upcoming terrorist attack and the theft of a drone from a company. But in the end, it might not be enough as NCIS find themselves paying a very high price for their efforts when one of their own is brutally murdered in Gibbs and Ari's battle with each other.... *Source:* [1]

Fornell: My second biggest mistake, Jethro? That's very dramatic. What was the first?
Gibbs: When you married my second wife.
Fornell: You could have warned me.
Gibbs: I did.
Fornell: In my own defense, I thought he was exaggerating. He wasn't.

McGee: Do you miss him as much as I do?
Kate: More.
McGee: I thought you said he was pig-headed. *('Pig-headed' is not the adjective used, but, I do not remember the correct adjective so, feel free to revise it.)*
Kate: That's part of his charm - he's like an X-rated Peter Pan.
Tony: "Me and Kate? Never happen."
McGee: "Why not?"
Tony: "She's too smart for that."

Gibbs: "Tony..."
Tony: "Yeah?"
Gibbs: "Go lie down before you pass out."
Tony: "I'm not going to pass out. I might cry a little, maybe feel sorry for myself, but DiNozzos do not pass out! I'm comin' Boss."

Tony: "You're never going to believe who's back in town."
Gibbs: "Ari."
Tony: "Maybe you will. Fornell said that he's here to..."
Gibbs: "Kill me. Yeah. I know. I just had coffee with him."
Tony: "So... what happened?"
Gibbs: "He tried to kill me."

Abby: "Hey. I had a weird dream about Tony last night."
Kate: "Ew! Not the one where you two are at the zoo and he..."
Abby: "No, he's fully clothed in this one. But he had blood all over his face. I woke up crying, Kate. I never cry. Never ever ever."

Gibbs: "Protection detail's over, Kate.
Tony: "You did good."
Gibbs: "For once, DiNozzo's right."
Kate: "Wow...I thought I'd die before I ever heard a comp...." (Kate is shot through the head and killed)

McGee: You don't look so hot.
Tony: Well, at least that's an improvement.
McGee: Over what?
Tony: According to Gibbs, I look like crap.

Source: [3]

Season 3 (Episodes 3.47- 3.70)

Originally broadcast between September 20, 2005 and May 16, 2006, the third season opens in the aftermath of "Twilight", with the entire team in shock and Gibbs on a vendetta to seek revenge for Kate's murder. Matters are complicated by the intervention of Gibbs' former lover and new NCIS Director Jenny Shepard, and Mossad Officer Ziva David.

Source: [1]

Original Air Date USA   September 20, 2005 – May 16, 2006 on CBS

Original Air Date German Language   March 16, 2006 – January 7, 2007 on Sat 1

Episodes Season 3

No.	German Title	US Title	Air Date USA	Air Date GER	Directed by	Written by
3.47	Das Duell – Teil 1	**Kill Ari (Part I)**	Sep 20, 2005	Mar 16, 2006	D.Smith	D.Bellisario

As the team struggles to come to terms with Kate Todd's brutal murder, Gibbs clashes with the new NCIS Director Jenny Shepard, who believes that Ari Haswari was not the one responsible for firing the bullet that killed Agent Todd due to the fact that there's no proof linking him to the crime. Ziva David, Ari's Mossad control officer, sides with the director, and causes problems when she arrives at the office, claiming that Ari is completely innocent. However, Ziva's motives for defending Ari become murky when she communicates with him and does not tell anyone in the NCIS office although Gibbs is aware and orders DiNozzo to tail her. Ari later returns and holding Gerald Jackson hostage yet again, kidnaps Ducky to divert the team's attention away from Ziva as he attempts to force Ducky into a meet. *Source:* [1]

```
Jenny: Jethro... I know it has been a difficult day for both of us...
Gibbs: That's what my DI used to say. Never believed him.


Tony: I don't want you to get pissed...
Gibbs: I thought you wanted me pissed.
Tony: I did...It was kind-of weird when you were being nice, not that your not
nice... I mean, ah...


Ziva: She wasn't attractive?
Tony: She was... but not to me...
Ziva: Then why did you imagine her naked?
```

Source: [3]

Episodes Season 3

No.	German Title	US Title	Air Date USA	Air Date GER	Directed by	Written by
3.48	Das Duell – Teil 2	**Kill Ari (Part 2)**	Sep 27, 2005	Mar 23, 2006	J.Whitmore, Jr.	D.Bellisario

Gibbs' determination to kill Ari increases after he mounts attacks against various members of the team in his sadistic game with Gibbs. Ari's control officer, Ziva David, begins to doubt Ari's innocence and agrees with Gibbs' plan to present Ari with the opportunity to kill him. Gibbs arrives at his house and to his surprise, Ari has been waiting for him, with Gibbs' rifle. But just before Ari can kill Gibbs, Ziva arrives and shoots Ari and killing him. It is only after the encounter between the three of them, that Gibbs discovers why Ziva was so quick to defend the murderer: she and Ari share the same father, Deputy Director Eli David of Mossad, making Ari Ziva's half-brother. After all is said and done, the team bid a sad farewell to Kate as she is laid to rest with civilian honors. Before resigning, former NCIS Director Tom Morrow approved Gibbs's request that Todd be awarded the Presidential Medal of Freedom. *Source: [1]*

Tony: Thanks for the pizza boss.
Gibbs: Thank the night shift... I swiped it from them.

Gibbs: We both can shut up.
Ziva: Espresso.Take it. It's not a bribe.
Tony: How long have you known I was......
Ziva: Following me? Since I left the Navy yard.
Tony: I don't think so.
Ziva: Blue sedan, you laid behind a white station wagon for a while, then a telephone van.You lost me at the traffic circle.
Tony: Okay, okay.You knew.
Ziva: *(offering him the coffee again)* Take it. It's chilly out here.You shouldn't feel bad, I was trained by the best.
Tony: You know, that's what I like about Mossad.
Ziva: Our training?
Tony: Your modesty.
Ziva: *(as Tony goes to throw away a pizza box)* Um, there's a slice in there! *(he gives it to her)* Todah.
Tony: Prego.
Ziva:......I lost my little sister, Taili, in a Hamas sucide bombing.She was sixteen and the best of us.Tali had compassion.
Tony: I'm sorry.
Ziva: After Tali's death, I was like Gibbs.All I wanted was revenge.
Tony: Is that why you joined Mossad?
Ziva: I was Mossad long before Tali's death.Old....
Tony: Family tradition.
Ziva: Israeli sense of duty.
Tony: But come on.Who recruited you? Father? Uncle? Brother? Boyfriend?
Ziva: Aunt, sister, lesbian lover.
Tony: You're good.You almost got me off the question. Almost.
Ziva: I volunteered.....Laila tov.
Tony: Buonanotte.

Gibbs: From now on, we're going to use phonetics like we did in the Marines.
Abby: Golf India Bravo Bravo Sierra?
Gibbs: What is it, Abbs?
Abby:Can I please go back to my lab;I'm flipping out up here with nothing to do
Gibbs: Fine, but--
Abby: I know, no leaving the building! Bravo Yankee Echo.
Gibbs: If I ask you something, Tobias are you going to lie to me?
Fornell: Depends on the question.
Gibbs: What's Ari Haswari's real mission here?
Fornell: I'm going to lie to you.Mossad lies to the CIA, they lie to us, I lie to you.I don't know who you lie to, being the bottom of the food chain......And not married. *Source: [3]*

Episodes Season 3

No.	German Title	US Title	Air Date USA	Air Date GER	Directed by	Written by
3.49	Der Mann in der Todeszelle	**Mind Games**	Oct 4, 2005	Mar 30. 2006	W.Webb	G.Schenck & F.Cardea

Death row prisoner Kyle Boone is a serial killer whom Gibbs arrested ten years ago. Having been placed on Death Row and due to be executed in a few days time, he insists that he will disclose the location of the missing bodies of his murder victims to Gibbs alone, forcing the reluctant team leader to meet with him. When Abby and McGee locate the place where the victims had been murdered, the team, assisted by Agent Cassidy, finds that the latest four victims in Boone's scrapbook had been killed in the last three years, meaning Boone has an accomplice. When Agent Cassidy goes missing, the team is forced into a desperate race against time to prevent her from becoming victim number five of the copycat killer. *Source:* [1]

Abby: You're not listening to a word I'm saying. I'm pregnant, McGee. Twins. Haven't told the father yet. It's Gibbs. I know it's wrong, but something about his silver hair just gets me all tingly inside

Tony: Excuse me for a second. I think I'm going to vomit

Abby: I'm joking, Tony. Except for the part about Gibbs' hair. That is really hot. McGee is ignoring me again

Tony: Easily fixable

(Tony hits McGee)

McGee: What?! What'd I do?

Tony: Stop ignoring Abby. She's sensitive

Ducky: Gibbs was a very different man 10 years ago.

Tony: You mean meaner?

Ducky: No, a lot like you, Tony!

McGee: Do we actually have knee pads Tony?

DiNozzo: I don't know Probie. Inventory is Kate's responsibility. Why don't you ask...

Ducky: Do you know the difference between good and bad cholesterol Tony?

Tony: No, but I'm guessing it has something to do with taste.

McGee: Uh, you two might wanna get busy. Gibbs is headed this way and he looks pissed.

Paula: Think he caved to the Governor?

Tony: No way.

McGee: No way, if Gibbs doesn't want to do something he doesn't.

Tony: No matter who's asking. (Gibbs gets his gun and badge out and walks off) Where you going boss?

Gibbs: Sussex State Prison to interview Kyle Boone. Be gone the rest of the day.

Paula: Yep, you two sure have him pegged.

Tony: The difference between ten years ago and today, Ducky? We have Gibbs' back.

Ducky: There's another difference, Tony.Ten years ago, Gibbs was a very different man.

Tony: You mean he was actually meaner?

Ducky: No, quite the opposite.He was......he was was a lot like you.

Source: [3]

Episodes Season 3

No.	German Title	US Title	Air Date USA	Air Date GER	Directed by	Written by
3.50	Sarg aus Eisen	**Silver War**	Oct 11, 2005	Apr 6, 2006	T.O'Hara	J.Lurie

A deceased Marine is found encased in a Civil-War era tomb at the Smithsonian museum and evidence later comes to light suggesting that he was probably buried alive. In the meantime, Ziva David joins NCIS as a liaison officer for Mossad and is assigned by the new director of NCIS, Jenny Shepard to Gibbs' team without his consent much to Gibbs's anger although Jenny insists that the team needs Ziva. She is forced to prove her worth to the team as they track down the people responsible for the Staff Sergeant's death, which is linked to a Civil War treasure. When Ducky and Ziva are placed in a difficult position, Ziva shows her value by saving both their lives. *Source:* [1]

Ducky: How do you tell a woman you have no mental recolection of her what-so-ever?
Palmer: I suppose one could always lie.
Ducky: Have you been spending time with Agent DiNozzo again?

Ziva: Who's the woman with Gibbs?
Tony: Yeah, once you're here long enough you'll figure it out.
Ziva: Is that his girlfriend?
Tony: I have no idea.
Ziva: You just told me....
Tony: Well, you'll figure out there are some things you don't ask about.

Source: [3]

No.	German Title	US Title	Air Date USA	Air Date GER	Directed by	Written by
3.51	Rollentausch	**Switch**	Oct 18, 2005	Apr 13, 2006	T.J.Wright	G.Grant

The team is called to investigate the murder of a Petty Officer who was gunned down while driving on a freeway. While visiting the sailor's commander to inform him of the death, the team discovers that another man claims to be the Petty Officer and that his identity may have been stolen. Secrets in both men's lives are revealed, but it is shrewd observations by Abby that end up solving the case. *Source:* [1]

Ziva: I'll drive, Tony.
Tony: No, no, no! Not gonna make that mistake again.
Ziva: Did you really think my driving was that terrible? Aside from the high speed and near misses?
Tony: Let's just say it's an acquired taste. Like regurgitated lunch.

Gibbs: I'd hate to start smacking you like I do DiNozzo
Abby: You wouldn't. You would?
Gibbs: It won't be on the head.

Ziva: Is he always this juvenile?
McGee: Only on the days of the week ending in day.

Ziva: Just to be clear, are there any more of these rules I should be aware of?
Gibbs: About 50 of them.
Ziva: And I don't suppose they're written down anywhere that I could...
Gibbs: NO.
Ziva: Then how am I supposed to...
Gibbs: My job is to teach them to you.

Source: [3]

Episodes Season 3

No.	German Title	US Title	Air Date USA	Air Date GER	Directed by	Written by
3.52	Voyeure im Netz	**The Voyeur's Web**	Oct 25, 2005	Apr 20, 2006	D.Smith	D.J.North

Jamie Carr, a Marine Sergeant's wife, is thought to have been abducted until Gibbs and his team found evidence to suggest that she may have been murdered live on the internet. Carr and her neighbor, Leanne Roberts, had been making money by running a live internet sex site while their husbands were deployed abroad. Roberts's body is later found but the team is still unable to find any trace of Carr. With the help of her new assistant, Charles Sterling who Director Shepard has hired for her, Abby determines that the video of Jamie might not be all it seems. *Source:* [1]

Ziva: Where did all these people come from?
Tony: Didn't you see the signs? It's yard sale day.
Ziva: I see. And do Marines sell their yards often?
McGee: No, it's actually when people gather stuff they don't want anymore, and sell it in their yards.
Ziva: Why would anyone want to buy somebody else's junk?
Tony: One man's junk is another man's treasure.
Ziva: In Israel, we have a saying. "Zevel Ze Zevel."
[Tony and McGee look at her, confused]
Ziva: Crap is crap.

McGee: Girlfriend is always emailing me these internet videos.She sent me one of this room last week.
DiNozzo: Why do I find that hard to believe?
McGee: What, you never get forwarded weird videos to your email?
DiNozzo: All the time.I meant the part about you having a girlfriend.

Abby: Oldest you've ever been with?
Tony: 26, my dry cleaner....You have a stuffed animal that farts?
Abby: Yeah! Cool, huh?
Tony: Yeah... in a disturbing kinda way...

McGee: Good news, boss. Naughty Naughty Neighbors has a webmaster
Gibbs Web what?
McGee: Webmaster. It's a person that is hired to design and update the page. His name is Carter Finch
Tony: Is this guy like a Super Fly cyber pimp?
McGee: Not exactly

Tony: I feel like I've just walked into page 8 of the IKEA catalogue...

Gibbs: The French wine in this particular region is terribly overrated.

Ziva: I've been meaning to ask you about that, Tony.How does a fifteen-year-old boy go about meeting a coquette?
McGee: She means rockette, boss.

Ziva: The odds of finding him off a list of that size is....
Gibbs: Better than the odd of you winning this argument.

Ziva: It could take days to search this place.
Tony: Why don't you tell Gibbs that, he loves our input.

Source: [3]

Episodes Season 3

No.	German Title	US Title	Air Date USA	Air Date GER	Directed by	Written by
3.53	Projekt „Honor"	**Honor Code**	Nov 1, 2005	Aug 13, 2006	C.Bucksey	C.Silber

Gibbs befriends a young boy after his father, a Lt. Commander, is kidnapped. The Lt. Commander had been working on a classified project named Honor and is the only person who has the code keys to the project. The release of the code keys can pose a serious threat to national security. Although the evidence gathered by Gibb's team suggests that the Lt. Commander was a part of the scheme, Gibbs believes otherwise due to the strong bond between the Lt. Commander and his son. *Source:* [1]

Jenny: Always admired your way with children. Ever think of having any of your own?
Gibbs: It that an offer Jen?
Jenny: No, it wasn't an offer, Jethro, it was merely an observation.

Gibbs: Dinner at the White House?
Jenny: A date, actually.
Gibbs: Must be an important guy for you to get all decked out.
Jenny: I would prefer it if you would just say you liked my dress.
Gibbs: I haven't decided yet.

Tony: Zach, hey. I'm Special Agent DiNozzo, you can call me Tony, okay? That's a smart thing to do, calling NCIS. Good boy. All right, I know this is really scary, but I want you to be brave. Can you do that? Okay, I want you to think back to what happened today. Try to remember the details. There's no wrong answer here.
Gibbs: What do we know?
Tony: Nothing. I think the kid's in shock.
Zach: No, I'm not. I'm waiting for Agent DiNozzo to ask me a question.
Tony: (about Zach) Do you see the way he's been acting around me?
Ziva: I think it's because he doesn't like you, Tony.
Tony: Kids dig me.
Ziva: No they don't. (Tony scoffs)
Tony: Zach.Zacharoo, buddy.Come on over here, man.I was gonna wait until tomarrow when everyone was here but considering what a brave little boy you've been and how much you've helped us, I'm gonna make you an honorary NCIS agent.
Zach: Thanks.I've gotta go to the head.
Ziva: (laughs) Yes, Tony, I was mistaken.Your way with children is only rivaled by your way with women.
Tony: He's under a lot of stress.

McGee: Have you ever considered the fact that Gibbs could be wrong this time?
Abby (gasps): "Ooh! McGee! Bite your tongue. Gibbs knows what he's doing, we just have to show him The Love.
Tony: We show him the love, Abby. We just don't want the bad guys to get away while we're doing it.

Ziva: The man is spick and Spam.
Tony: The saying is 'spick and span'. Spam is lunch meat.
Ziva: Oh. What exactly is 'span' then?
Tony: Span is.....I'll get back to you on that.

McGee: How many people owe you favors?
Ziva: How many dates does Tony go on a month.

Source: [3]

Episodes Season 3

No.	German Title	US Title	Air Date USA	Air Date GER	Directed by	Written by
3.54	Goldherz	**Under Covers**	Nov 8, 2005	Aug 20, 2006	L.Lipstadt	L.D.Zlotoff

When it is discovered that two married assassins, who were fatally wounded in a car crash, were planning an assassination at the United States Marine Corps Birthday Ball, Gibbs sends Ziva and Tony to pose as the married assassins in order to find out who the couple had planned to assassinate and who had hired them. After the team finds out that the couple were expecting a baby and may have been planning to retire, they realize that the assassination plot could have been a set-up and that the married assassins were potentially the real targets. Meanwhile, an attraction between Tony and Ziva surfaces. *Source:* [1]

Tony: Sweetheart? You know what I could really use right now?
Ziva: Some deodorant?

Tony: Maybe she didn't know.
Ziva: Oh, she knew.
Tony: Then why do this job risking to lose the baby?
Ziva: Maybe she needed the money.
Tony: Yeah, kids are expensive...
Ziva: And bullets are cheap.

Ducky: Though it may be common knowledge that I talk to my patients, unfortunately to date, none of them have ever answered me back.
Gibbs: Listen harder.

Source: [3]

No.	German Title	US Title	Air Date USA	Air Date GER	Directed by	Written by
3.55	In der Falle	**Frame Up**	Nov 22, 2005	Aug 27, 2006	T.J.Wright	L.Walsh

A pair of legs are found on a Marine base, and the team is dumbfounded and shellshocked when every piece of evidence in a murder points towards Tony as the prime suspect. In an effort to help their colleague, the team compiles a list of people who may have grudges against Tony, providing them with a long list of suspects. Abby is upset that she may have incriminated Tony through the forensic evidence she provided and refuses to give up until she's proved his innocence. *Source:* [1]

Ziva: What do women try to achieve by cracking eggs on a man's car?
McGee: Most men love their cars, it's a way of saying "You broke my heart, I break yours."
Ziva: In Israel, we just shoot men who are untrue.

Ziva: She's probably passed on by now.
McGee: The term is passed out.
Ziva: Whatever, the girl is tired.

Ziva: The personnel in the evidence garage!
Tony: What about 'em?
Ziva: They hate you.
McGee: She's right; you never wait your turn to check in evidence.
Ziva: And women don't appreciate being called "baggie bunnies."

Gibbs: Ass kissing on the hill is a skill
Jenny: So is castration.
Gibbs: I wear a cup.

Abby: We have to save him Gibbs.Because if he goes to court with fingerprint and his bite mark on the leg, Tony's gonna go to prison for the rest of his life.And I'll be the one that put him there.

Source: [3]

Episodes Season 3

No.	German Title	US Title	Air Date USA	Air Date GER	Directed by	Written by
3.56	Drei Kugeln	**Probie**	Nov 29, 2005	Sep 3, 2006	T.O'Hara	G.Schenck & F.Cardea

While the team is on protective detail for the Chief of Naval Operations, McGee spots an argument taking place in an alleyway. He shoots one of the men, who he believed was aiming a gun at him. The deceased turns out to be a D.C. Metro police detective who was working undercover. When the team is unable to find any weapon or bullets left behind by anyone other than McGee, it appears that McGee may have made a probie mistake. McGee begins to doubt himself but Gibbs is suspicious of the detective's meeting, which took place that night. After speaking to the decedent's partner, the team realizes that McGee's story may be more accurate than any of them thought. *Source:* [1]

Gibbs Rule #8: Never take anything for granted.

Tony: McGee, the first time I shot at someone, I wet my pants.
McGee: Really?
Tony: Really. If you tell anyone, I will slap you silly.

Source: [3]

No.	German Title	US Title	Air Date USA	Air Date GER	Directed by	Written by
3.57	Boot Camp Babes	**Model Behavior**	Dec 13, 2005	Sep 10, 2006	S.Cragg	D.J.Nort

A supermodel is found dead after having overdosed on phencyclidine at a Marine base, where the reality TV show in which she was participating was being filmed. Her ex-boyfriend is also found dead in a motel nearby having overdosed on heroin, leading the team to believe that their deaths may have been related to their relationship. However, when it is discovered that the Marine drill instructor in charge of the TV show was romantically linked to the dead supermodel, the team look closer at the others involved in the show. When the Marine boyfriend begins to overdose on the same thing that killed his girlfriend, it appears that someone may have disapproved of the relationship, even going to extreme lengths to end it. *Source:* [1]

Supermodel: Anything else we can help you with? Like some hair tips for your girlfriend here? *(referring to Ziva)*
McGee: No, I, uh, think that about covers it. But if you can remember anything else that might help, please give us a call. *(hands her his card)*
Ziva: It's called a business card. Maybe you can have one of the Marines read it to you?

Source: [3]

No.	German Title	US Title	Air Date USA	Air Date GER	Directed by	Written by
3.58	Die Spur des Geldes	**Boxed In**	Jan 11, 2006	Sep 17, 2006	D.Smith	D.Coen

While investigating a naval stockyard for a container with illegal weapons, Tony and Ziva are ambushed and forced to take cover in a container, where they subsequently become locked in. Gibbs, McGee and Abby attempt to search for them with the help of the port security office. Meanwhile, Tony and Ziva discover that the crates of DVD movies inside the container served as a cover for hidden crates, which contain million of dollars of counterfeit money. But they both find themselves in a gunfight after the container is later taken away to a warehouse guarded by terrorists, forcing Gibbs and McGee into a race against time to find their location before Tony and Ziva end up dead. . *Source:* [1]

Gibbs: They were caught in the cross fire.
McGee: Boss you don't think......well...should we put divers in the water?
Gibbs: They're not in the water. McGee, if they were in the water they'd be dead.If they dead I'd know about it.

Source: [3]

Episodes Season 3

No.	German Title	US Title	Air Date USA	Air Date GER	Directed by	Written by
3.59	Ein langer Sonntag	**Deception**	Jan 17, 2006	Sep 24, 2006	D.Smith	D.Coen

A Navy Lt. Commander, who was in charge of a shipment of nuclear weapons, is thought to have been abducted leading to Gibbs and his team being called in on a Sunday to investigate. The team discovers that the Lt. Commander had had a meeting earlier in the day at a shopping center and that she did volunteer work at an organization which combats online pedophilia, meaning that her abductor might not have been a terrorist but a pedophile she was tracking. *Source:* [1]

Gibbs Rule #3: Never be unreachable.

Ziva: Why don't I think what she said is a good thing?
Tony: Because you're a better agent than you are a driver.

Abby: Thank you sir!
Gibbs: Don't call me sir.
Abby: Thank you ma'am!

Tony: Do you know what I like about coming to work on a Sunday?
Ziva: Relaxed dress code?
Tony: Actually no, it offers us the unique chance to get a glimpse into the private life of our co workers.
Ziva: Except I have no interest in your life.

Source: [3]

No.	German Title	US Title	Air Date USA	Air Date GER	Directed by	Written by
3.60	Schläfer	**Light Sleeper**	Jan 24, 2006	Oct 1, 2006	C.Bucksey	C.Silber

When the Korean wives of two Marines are murdered, Gibbs and his team are sent in to investigate. Since signs of domestic abuse were evident at the crime scene, they suspect that the killer is one of the women's husbands. The sudden disappearance of Yoon Dawson, a friend of the two victims, makes her husband a suspect in the case. However, the team soon discovers that Yoon is not all she seems, and that she and her two dead friends might have been in America for reasons other than having Marine husbands. *Source:* [1]

Gibbs: What did the urine tell you Abby?
Abby: Oh, all kinds of stuff, we had a really good talk.

McGee: Boss, Did you find her?
Gibbs: Yes McGee, She's hiding in my coffee cup.

Gibbs: Sign of an unhappy marriage.
Ziva: Funny. I think it looks like a hole in the wall.

Tony: It's like my father used to tell me: "Be careful who you marry, Anthony. You never know if they're gonna turn out to be a maniac serial killer.
McGee: Your father actually said that to you?
Tony: No, but I'm pretty sure he thought it.
Ziva: He probably knew your taste in women.

Gibbs: Tony, Ziva, what happened back there with that bomb.....I just want you to know....
Tony: You don't have to say it, boss, we know how you feel about us.
Ziva: We are a team, Gibbs. It's what we do.
Gibbs: I was going to say if either one of you two wing-nuts ever disobey a direct order again, I'll kill you myself.
Tony: That's our boss!

Source: [3]

Episodes Season 3

No.	German Title	US Title	Air Date USA	Air Date GER	Directed by	Written by
3.61	Kopfsache	**Head Case**	Feb 7, 2006	Oct 8, 2006	D.Smith	G.Schenck & F.Cardea

While conducting a raid on an automotive chop shop run by Marines, the team finds a severed head in one of the cars. The head belonged to a Navy Captain, who was thought to have been cremated. Their investigation leads them to the discovery of a scheme involving the illegal sale of human body parts, which came from stolen bodies. *Source:* [1]

Jenny: Do you think it would be inappropriate if, as Director, I went in there and slapped that smile off her face?
Gibbs: Yeah, it would. That's what you have me for.

Tony: Sleepless in Seattle?
Ziva: That was about voodoo?
Tony: No, but the first time I saw it, scared the bejezus out of me.

Tony: You thinking what I'm thinking?
McGee: Yeah, that we've just walked into an episode of the X-files.

Source: [3]

No.	German Title	US Title	Air Date USA	Air Date GER	Directed by	Written by
3.62	Familiengeheimnis	**Family Secrets**	Feb 28, 2006	Oct 15, 2006	J.Withmore jr.	S.D.Binder

An ambulance explodes and practically disintegrates the body of William Danforth, a deceased Marine it was carrying. A DNA analysis performed on a piece of body tissue informs the team that the body does not belong to Danforth. The team suspects that Danforth's best friend, who was a bomb expert, helped Danforth fake his death in order to leave the Marine Corps. When Danforth is discovered to have been a recipient of a donor organ, the team realizes that the body may in fact be Danforth's after all, and they are forced to examine reasons as to why someone may have wanted to disguise that the body was his. *Source:* [1]

Gibbs: Any chance of getting the call logs?
Abby: I'd have a better chance of getting McGee to wear a a Speedo to church.

Gibbs: DiNozzo, shut up!
Tony: Shutting up, Boss!

Source: [3]

No.	German Title	US Title	Air Date USA	Air Date GER	Directed by	Written by
3.63	Bärenjäger	**Ravenous**	Mar 7, 2006	Oct 22, 2006	T.Wright	R.C.Arthur

A Marine is suspected to have been eaten by a bear after a group of teenagers found his dog tags in bear feces in a national forest. However, autopsy reveals that the Marine was killed by a blade before his corpse was eaten by a bear. Evidence also shows that he was camping with a woman, who is now missing. The team's search for the woman and the Marine's killer leads them to a realization that their case may be linked to several women of similar appearance who have been found dead in the national forest. The team realizes that locals may know more than they have been telling. *Source:* [1]

Abby: I was just about to call Tony and McGee.I think they were having sex.
Ziva: (surprised) Tony and McGee?
Abby: No!

Ziva: Not a big fan of nature huh?
Tony: Oh.. I'm a big fan of nature as long as it's on TV.

Source: [3]

Episodes Season 3

No.	German Title	US Title	Air Date USA	Air Date GER	Directed by	Written by
3.64	Der letzte Sonnenuntergang	**Bait**	Mar 14, 2006	Nov 12, 2006	T.O'Hara	L.Walsh

The teenage son of a Marine Major holds his classmates hostage inside a classroom by threatening them with a bomb strapped to his chest. Gibbs and his team arrive on scene but are unable to get audio and video of the situation inside the classroom so Gibbs puts himself in danger by offering himself as a hostage. While Tony takes charge of the team, the boy demands that his mother be brought to the classroom by sunset, but the team discovers that she has been dead for a year. Gibbs suspects that the boy is not acting alone when he sees an earwig in the boy's ear. *Source:* [1]

```
Tony: How long?
McGee: Depends.They could be using counter attack software.If they're using a
sophisticated encryption system.It could be one hundred twenty-eight even two
hundred fifty-six bit...
Tony: Probie!
McGee: On it, boss!............Tony!
Ziva: What?
Tony: He called me boss.
Ziva: Yeah, he'll never live it down.
Tony: Nope.
```

Source: [3]

No.	German Title	US Title	Air Date USA	Air Date GER	Directed by	Written by
3.65	Tot im Eis	**Iced**	Apr 4, 2006	Nov 19, 2006	D.Smith	D.Coen

NCIS is called to investigate a dead Marine First Sergeant found in a frozen lake. The discovery of three more dead men in the lake leads Gibbs to the underworld of an international street gang, which may threaten the safety of the team. The team finds a link between the dead men and a one-year-old case concerning the accidental shooting of a Marine by the gang. *Source:* [1]

```
Ducky: Yes, I once performed an autopsy on a man who drowned in his kitchen
sink. Yes, apparently, he couldn't remove the drain plug and attempted to use
his teeth.

McGee: Something wrong, boss?
Gibbs: Just admiring your feminine glow.
```

Source: [3]

No.	German Title	US Title	Air Date USA	Air Date GER	Directed by	Written by
3.66	Das Leck	**Untouchable**	Apr 18, 2006	Nov 26, 2006	L.Libman	G.Schenck & F.Cardea

Due to suspicions of a mole working inside the Pentagon, Tony and Ziva are charged with interviewing members of the Pentagon's cryptography department. When one of their interviewees is found dead in her home, the team investigates her apparent suicide. While the cryptography department is immediately locked down, Abby uses forensic science to prove that a second person was in the room when the gun was fired.. *Source:* [1]

```
Abby: Rough night?
Ziva: Is there any other kind with Gibbs?

Abby: Stop being so "Palmer," Jimmy.
```

Source: [3]

Episodes Season 3

No.	German Title	US Title	Air Date USA	Air Date GER	Directed by	Written by
3.67	Typisch Montag	**Bloodbath**	Apr 25, 2006	Dec 3, 2006	D.Smith	S.D.Binder

After a room at a Navy lodging facility is found to have blood and fragments of flesh scattered throughout, the team is called to investigate. However, evidence suggests that it was a set-up crime scene. Meanwhile, Abby returns from court after giving testimony in an embezzlement trial and is attacked in her lab. Gibbs puts Abby into protective custody with the team while they look for the person targeting Abby, who appears to be a stalker. It was discovered that the defendant in the trial had used some of the ill-gotten money to hire a hit man to target Abby. It was Abby, who had been armed with pepper spray, brass knuckles and a taser gun, who had subdued the hit man, and helped to get the defendant arrested. *Source:* [1]

McGee: Did you request this specific room when you called the lodge?
Lillian: No we asked for the one with the eviscerated squirrels, but this was all they had.
Frank: What the h*** kind of question is that?
Gibbs: Our last one.

McGee: Or, maybe it was just a lab accident. I mean, really, who would wanna kill Abby?
Ziva: You know that's true. It's not like someone was after Tony.
McGee: Now that's a suspect list I wouldn't want to run down again.
Tony: Ya! Ha-ha! Ha-ha! I think the joke's over. We get it.

Source: [3]

No.	German Title	US Title	Air Date USA	Air Date GER	Directed by	Written by
3.68	Brüder	**Jeopardy**	May 2, 2006	Dec 10, 2006	J.Whitmore jr.	D.J.North

NCIS investigates the death of a suspect who was in Ziva's custody but the investigation turns critical when the dead man's brother kidnaps Director Shepard and threatens to kill her unless the seized evidence and his brother are returned, unaware that his brother is actually dead. While Ducky works to find the man's cause of death, the team desperately searches for their Director before it's too late. Note: The suspect dies in an elevator. In the previous week's episode, Abby tells of the low frequency of people dying in elevators. *Source:* [1]

Tony: Look, we all know that Ziva has crazy Ninja skills, but I mean, she's got some self control right? Not a lot, but some. Never mind.

Gibbs: You sure this is the stupidest thing you've ever done, DiNozzo?

Ducky: I've been traveling to crime scenes for a great many years, but I can say with complete confidence this is the shortest commute I have ever had.
Jimmy: And one of the first times I didn't get us lost.
Ducky: True.

Jenny: Gibbs thinks of me as a wife.
James: See.
Jenny: He's had three.

Abby: Oh my God. I've turned into my Uncle Larry.

Ziva: I didn't touch him... Hardly at all.

Tony: I'm afraid you'll put the Vulcan death grip on me.

Source: [3]

Episodes Season 3

No.	German Title	US Title	Air Date USA	Air Date GER	Directed by	Written by
3.69	Fünfzehn Jahre	**Hiatus (Part I)**	May 9, 2006	Dec 17, 2006	D.Smith	D.Bellisario

A bomb explodes as Gibbs contacts an undercover government agent on a suspicious foreign ship, killing the agent and placing Gibbs in a coma, in which he has flashbacks of the murder of his wife Shannon and daughter Kelly many years earlier, and his wounding in Desert Storm. Meanwhile, Tony becomes the temporary head of the investigation team as the group attempts to track down Pinpin Pula, a missing crew member of the ship, suspected to be an Abu Sayyaf member. Gibbs awakens from his coma at the end of the episode with no memory of Ducky, who is in the room with him. *Source:* [1]

Ducky: I sat on a bomb once. No twice. The first time I was young, the second time I was foolish.
Palmer: Why would you sit on a bomb?
Ducky: I just told you. I was young and foolish. Haven't you been listening?

Dr.Todd: How well do you know Gibbs?
Jenny: He was my mentor at NCIS; he taught me most of what I know.
Dr.Todd: Yet you're his boss.
Jenny: Jethro's a great field agent. He's a great team leader. And he deals more efficiently with difficult politicians than I do.
Dr.Todd: Then why isn't he the...
Jenny: He shoots them.

Abby: McGee said that Gibbs was in a bomb blast. He tried to sound really calm, but I could hear the fear in his voice and he should be afraid, for Gibbs to be brought to the hospital in the ambulance could not be good. I had to come see for myself and my hearse got a flat as usual so, um, I got in a cab to go to the airport and then I realised that, that by the time I got to the terminal and, and I bought a ticket and then I went through security and then I flew to Norfolk and then I got a cab here it would be better just to stay in the cab that I was in so I did that, it cost a lost of, you know what it doesn't matter what it cost because this is Gibbs we're talking about. I can't believe that he's hurt he is never hurt, not hurt enough to go to a hospital. He has to be dying to even go see a doctor. Oh my God. He isn't dying is he? I dunno what I would do. Positive thoughts, positive thoughts, positive thoughts. Ok, I know the rule is that you have to be family to go into Emergency, at least that's what they said when Uncle Charlie got his leg caught in a nurtia trap, but Gibbs and me, we're tighter than blood. I know you need ID, I have ID in here. Um, I work at NCIS, uh, forensics, and, uh, ballistics, chemical analysis and DNA typing. Uh, here, um, that's me. I promise, I just, I had to be in court that day but I swear, that is me.

Tony: Shouldn't he be awake by now?
Jenny: You know Gibbs. He keeps his own schedule. Do you know what REM is?
Tony: Sure. Rapid Eye Movement. It happens when you're asleep and dreaming.
Jenny: That's what it looks like he's doing now.
Tony: Oh well, that's gotta be a good sign right?
Jenny: If it isn't a nightmare.

Tony: This is so "Usual Suspects".
Ziva: Tony, your dying words will be, "I've seen this film".

McGee: On it boss!
Tony: I do love it when he calls me boss.
Ziva: Is that why you're being nice to him?
Tony: I'm not being nice. Lugging foot lockers is probie work.

Source: [3]

Episodes Season 3

No.	German Title	US Title	Air Date USA	Air Date GER	Directed by	Written by
3.70	Semper Fi	**Hiatus (Part II)**	May 16, 2006	Jan 7, 2007	D.Smith	D.Bellisario

Director Shepard contacts Gibbs' NCIS mentor and partner, Mike Franks in hopes of helping an amnesiac Gibbs regain his memory as only he knows the details to an impending terrorist attack. She also delves into Gibbs' past and shares with Ducky about his murdered wife and daughter. Ziva, who had appeared nonchalant about Gibbs' situation, visits Gibbs in a desperate and emotional attempt to revive his memory by telling him about their shared connection with Ari. Meanwhile, Tony and the team discover Pinpin Pula wants to blow up the ship Cape Fear. Gibbs recovers his memory and tries to stop the terrorist attack, but fails because his superiors ignore his warnings. Finally, Gibbs hands his badge to Tony and resigns before heading to Mexico to stay at Franks's house.
Source: [1]

```
Gibbs Rule #11: When the job is done, walk away.

Tony: My gut tells me we're missing something.
Ziva: Gibbs?
Tony: Yeah. Gibbs.

Gibbs: What can I do?
Ziva: Remember!
Gibbs: I've been trying to since I woke up in this room!
Ziva: Well try harder! ... That's a start.
Gibbs: What is?
Ziva: The old Gibbs' stare. You gave it to all of us; McGee, Tony, me!
Gibbs: What are you talking about?

Abby: Can you imagine how scray that would be? To lose the last fifteen years
of your life.
McGee: Oh, man!
Abby: What?
McGee: I'd still be in highschool.
Abby: Uh, yuck! Zits, braces. rageing hormones.
McGee: Yeah, used to walk around all day with a notebook in front of my.....
Abby: In front of your what, McGee?
McGee: (pointing to the computer) The laundry room is off.It should actually be
3.962 meters wide, no twenty-six.
Abby: (fixs it) Better?
McGee: Yeah.Gotta be accurate.
Abby: Absolutly.So was it one of these tiny spiral notebooks? Or one of those
big three ring binder kinda ones, Timmy?
McGee: And where were you fifteen years ago, Abby?
Abby: So where did you find Gibbs?
McGee: Afraid I'm gonna find out.... (Abby hits him) What was that for?
Abby: Distracting me.
McGee: I was not distracting.....
Abby: (pointing at the computer) Gibbs.
McGee: Between the drier and the bulkhead......Little closer to the
bulkhead.Now the autopsty report indicates that Gableeb was sitting on the
bomb.
Abby: Which consisted of one hundred-thirteen grands of semtex.
McGee: Wow.You can compute the amount of semtex used?
Abby: I'm a scientist, McGee.I can compute anything acurtly, including the sizr
of the notebook required to.....
McGee: Stop.
```

Source: [3]

Season 4 (Episodes 4.71- 4.94)

The fourth season of NCIS was originally broadcast between September 19, 2006 and May 22, 2007. Special Agent Gibbs left NCIS at the end of season 3 after a terrorist attack had been successful because his superiors did not heed his warnings in time. The team is now led by DiNozzo for a short time until Gibbs' eventual return. New characters introduced in this season are Michelle Lee, who was briefly on DiNozzo's team and was transferred to the legal department upon Gibbs' return, and (already in the final episodes of season 3) Gibbs' former boss & mentor Mike Franks, both as recurring characters. Also, albeit later in the season, Army CID Lieutenant Colonel Hollis Mann is introduced as another love interest for Gibbs.

Source: [1]

Original Air Date USA	September 19, 2006 – May 22, 2007 on CBS
Original Air Date German Language	March 4, 2007 – November 18, 2007 on Sat 1

Episodes Season 4

No.	German Title	US Title	Air Date USA	Air Date GER	Directed by	Written by
4.71	Schalom	**Shalom**	Sep 19, 2006	Mar 4, 2007	W.Webb	J.C.Kelley

After witnessing a Mossad agent perform an assassination, which was not authorized by Mossad, Ziva is suspected by the FBI to be a double agent. Now a fugitive and on the run, Ziva is forced to ask for help from Gibbs, who is in Mexico after retiring from NCIS. Tony finds his leadership skills being tested to the limit as he leads the team to search for Ziva and to prove her innocence before the FBI can arrest her. *Source:* [1]

```
Tony: "Let's roll. Hey, no, this is my team now, Gibbs. My rules. And DiNozzo's
Rule #1 is I don't sit on the sidelines when my people are in trouble. You got
a problem with that? Just remember whose got a badge and who is a civilian."
Gibbs: "Done?" (He headslaps Tony)
Tony: "Yeah."
Gibbs: "I was going to say get McGee and I'll meet you there."
Tony: "You know I could arrest you for striking a Federal officer."
Gibbs: "I know that."
Tony: "Alright. Just so you know."

Tony: "You listen to Yanni. And you have an unauthorized game on your
computer."
McGee: "Okay, it's your game Tony."
Tony: "You shouldn't have beaten my high score."

Tony: "That's not my point! Six months ago you were convinced that I killed a
woman and chopped off her legs!"
Sacks: "Well, I'm still not convinced that you didn't."
Tony: "Exactly."
Sacks: "So, Ziva David is being framed... by who?"
Tony: "Well, that's what I intend to find out."
Sacks: "Hah! Good luck with that."
```

Source: [3]

Episodes Season 4

No.	German Title	US Title	Air Date USA	Air Date GER	Directed by	Written by
4.72	Auf der Flucht	**Escaped**	Sep 26, 2006	Mar 11, 2007	D.Smith	S.D.Binder & C.Silber

A former Petty Officer, convicted of murder, escapes from prison and forces F.B.I. Special Agent Fornell to reopen his case in order to find the real culprit whilst claiming his own innocence. Fornell asks for Gibbs' help, who is reinstated as an NCIS agent by Director Shepard. To his former team's disappointment, Gibbs insists that the reinstatement is only temporary. The team soon finds discrepancies in the Petty Officer's case and that he may have been framed. *Source:* [1]

```
Ziva: You know, you used to be a nice person, McGee. I think sitting at Tonys
desk is affecting your personality.
Tony: For the better! McGee picked up a girl all by himself.
Ziva: Yeah, at a funeral!
Tony: You didnt tell me that.
```

Source: [3]

No.	German Title	US Title	Air Date USA	Air Date GER	Directed by	Written by
4.73	Schnelle Liebe	**Singled Out**	Oct 3, 2006	Mar 18, 2007	T.O'Hara	D.J.North

Gibbs returns to NCIS and leads his team to investigate the kidnapping of a Navy Lieutenant, who is a computer specialist. They discover that the Lieutenant had used her military knowledge to profile potential husbands and was attending speed dating events. When they suspect that the kidnapper may continue attending the event in order to avoid suspicion, Ziva goes undercover at a speed-dating event to identify him. In addition, Tony is offered a promotion - his own team, as a reward for his performance as team leader while Gibbs was retired - but declines, and remains in Gibbs' team.. *Source:* [1]

```
Ziva: "I look like a dork."
Tony: "Yeah, that's the idea."

Gibbs: "You're a geek, Ziva David. Not mentally deranged."

Ziva: Ninety-second dates? I thought you were kidding me, Gibbs.
Gibbs: Youll do fine, Ziva. I had marriages shorter than that.
Ziva: Ha! Im beginning to understand why.
```

Source: [3]

No.	German Title	US Title	Air Date USA	Air Date GER	Directed by	Written by
4.74	Der größte Köder	**Faking It**	Oct 10, 2006	Mar 25, 2007	T.J.Wright	S.Brennan

A Petty Officer is found dead in his car with "NCIS" written in blood on the seat. The investigation becomes complicated when Homeland Security claims that the Russian Spy suspected of killing the officer is working for them. *Source:* [1]

```
Tony (looking at McGee asleep on the table): "Do you have any superglue Abbs?"
Gibbs: "What did I tell you about that DiNozzo?"
Tony: "That, next time, the skin might not grow back?!"

Abby: So I have a pirstine bullet sample fired from our suspect's Thirty-
eight.All I need is the bullet you pulled from him. I'll make a match and we'll
send the bad guys wherever the bad guys go when we catch 'em! Where do the bad
guys go when we catch 'em?
```

Source: [3]

Episodes Season 4

No.	German Title	US Title	Air Date USA	Air Date GER	Directed by	Written by
4.75	Die Verlobten	**Dead and Unburied**	Oct 17, 2006	Apr 1, 2007	C.Bucksey	N.Scovell

When a missing Lance Corporal is found dead in a vacant house, the NCIS team discovers that he was buried in the backyard and then exhumed. They learn about his identity and that he was to be deployed to Iraq, but he never showed up for duty. The investigation leads them to a new clue - he had two fiancées. Abby runs the DNA samples from the two women to find out if the DNA is a match to the soil found on the dead man's body. *Source:* [1]

Abby: "You know what they say about guys with big hands and big feet right."
Ducky: "What?"
Abby: "They're clowns."

Ziva: "McGee. Give me your flashlight."
McGee: "Why? You didn't bring your own?"
Ziva: "It's too heavy. It pulls my pants down."

Abby: "Aww, you shaved your moustache! I liked you with a little hair on your face."
Gibbs: "I still have my eyebrows."
Abby: "Good point."

Abby: And his underwear are boxer breifs like you wear Gibbs.
Gibbs: Youre fishing, Abbs.
Abby: So are they regular boxers? Trunks? Nothing?

Source: [3]

No.	German Title	US Title	Air Date USA	Air Date GER	Directed by	Written by
4.76	Halloween	**Witch Hunt**	Oct 31, 2006	Apr 8, 2007	J.Whitmore jr.	S.Kriozere

It's Halloween and the NCIS team is busy investigating a ransom case. A Marine's daughter has been kidnapped after the kidnapper attacked the Marine in his home. The investigation leads them to a fact that the couple has been separated. They decide to focus on the wife's ex-boyfriend, after learning that the woman is the one who destroyed their marriage. Meanwhile, McGee and Tony are stunned by Abby's Halloween costume. *Source:* [1]

Tony: Last time I did Halloween I was an astronaut. The neighborhood I grew up in, well it wasn't really a neighborhood; there were these estates with mansions smack dab in the middle of them. And really long driveways. Made Halloween very tricky. It's a lot of walking. My feet were tired that night. Dogs were barking.
McGee: Yeah, I gotta imagine it really sucks growing up rich like that.
Tony: My costume was fantastic though. Wicked awesome. I was a spaceman. No ventilation though. I was sweating like Roger Federer after a five-set tie breaker. And stinky. Stinky like cheese. But man what a haul. I made off with more candy than I could carry.
McGee: I hope this story's coming to an end soon.
Tony: But when I got home, my old man made me throw it all away. Even the apples.
McGee: He was concerned about your teeth.
Tony: Oh... no. I made my astronaut suit out of one of this $3000 designer ski suits.
McGee: Ouch.
Tony: I don't think I sat down again 'til Christmas.

Source: [3]

Episodes Season 4

No.	German Title	US Title	Air Date USA	Air Date GER	Directed by	Written by
4.77	Der Hintermann	**Sandblast**	Nov 7, 2006	Apr 15, 2007	D.Smith	R.Palm

When a Marine Colonel dies in an explosion at a military golf course, the NCIS team must investigate a suspected terrorist attack with the help from the Army Criminal Investigative Division (CID). The CIA gives them a lead to an abandoned warehouse, but it turns out to be a trap - the warehouse is set to explode. McGee uses his computer skills to break into the secret government files to uncover the terrorist cell while Tony attempts to stop the Marine Colonel's son from joining the Marines to avenge his father's death. *Source:* [1]

```
Lt.Col.Mann: If this is gonna be a pissing match you'd better bring an
umbrella.
Tony: Got something boss. What'd I miss?
Ziva: Gibbs just found his fourth ex-wife.

McGee: "That's pretty clever, Boss. How did you figure that out?"
Gibbs: "Too much time around you."
```
Source: [3]

No.	German Title	US Title	Air Date USA	Air Date GER	Directed by	Written by
4.78	Einmal ein Held	**Once a Hero**	Nov 14, 2006	Apr 22, 2007	T.J.Wright	S.Brennan

When an honored Marine veteran is found dead in a hotel, the NCIS team must find out what happened to him. Soon they realize that the Marine didn't commit suicide and that he was homeless. After going through his personal belongings, they find compromising evidence against him, and Gibbs is determined to prove the man's innocence. *Source:* [1]

```
Gibbs: There's more than one reason to kiss a girl.
Tony: There is?
Jeanne: Has anyone ever told you, you're an idiot.
Tony: Yeah, my boss, all the time.
```
Source: [3]

No.	German Title	US Title	Air Date USA	Air Date GER	Directed by	Written by
4.79	Die kleine Schwester	**Twisted Sister**	Nov 21, 2006	Apr 29, 2007	T.J.Wright	S.Brennan

When McGee's younger sister Sarah (played by Troian Bellisario) shows up disoriented and bloodied, believing that she might have killed someone at his door in the middle of the night, McGee takes matters into his hands, beginning his own independent investigation but Sarah claims she's innocent although her memory of the last few hours is blank. While McGee works on figuring out what happened to his sister, the NCIS team is investigating a case of a Navy sailor, who is somehow connected to McGee's sister. Both Tony and Abby are busy with love problems, while McGee turns out to have another secret. *Source:* [1]

No.	German Title	US Title	Air Date USA	Air Date GER	Directed by	Written by
4.80	Die Mumie	**Smoked**	Nov 28, 2006	May 6, 2007	B.Webb	J.C.Kelley

A dead man in a chimney chute on a marine base leads the team to discover a serial killer's burial ground. They believe that the dead man was the serial killer until Abby uncovers something which proves he may actually be a victim. Meanwhile, Tony helps the director with a special project and makes time for his girlfriend as well while Ducky talks to Gibbs about how he felt betrayed when Gibbs left and after a heart-to-heart the two eventually repair their friendship. *Source:* [1]

```
Gibbs Rule #22: Never, ever interrupt Gibbs in interrogation.
```
Source: [3]

Episodes Season 4

No.	German Title	US Title	Air Date USA	Air Date GER	Directed by	Written by
4.81	Sabotage	**Driven**	Dec 12, 2006	May 13, 2007	D.Smith	N.Scovell & J.C.Kelley

A woman is found dead in a classified robotic vehicle she was working on developing. Although it initially looks like suicide, when Abby puts the vehicle through some tests, it nearly takes her life as well. They discover that someone rigged the vehicle to kill the passenger and make it appear to be suicide. They discover that the woman who was killed was not the intended target. Meanwhile, Tony visits the hospital to see his girlfriend and continues working on special projects for the Director. Ziva notices Tony getting calls from the hospital and begins worrying that he is sick. *Source: 1*

```
Tony: I think you should go and check the bedroom. That is... unless you want
me to come with you and help...What?
Ziva: Just wondering if offering to take me to a bedroom constitutes sexual
harassment?
Tony: Well, if you have to ask then it's not harassment.
```
Source: 3

No.	German Title	US Title	Air Date USA	Air Date GER	Directed by	Written by
4.82	Verdacht	**Suspicion**	Jan 16, 2007	May 20, 2007	C.Bucksey	S.Brennan

When a Marine is murdered in a small town hotel room, NCIS is called in to investigate. However, the local Sheriff's department already cleaned up the crime scene and performed an autopsy. They also have a suspect - an Iraqi national who just moved to town a few months earlier. *Source: 1*

```
Gibbs: "Give me some news, Abs"
Abby: "I'm not pregnant"
Gibbs: "Too much information"

Tony: Probie, i have a pimple on my left buttox that is a better writer than
you.
```
Source: 3

No.	German Title	US Title	Air Date USA	Air Date GER	Directed by	Written by
4.83	Giftgas	**Sharif Returns**	Jan 23, 2007	May 27, 2007	T.O'Hara	S.D.Binder

When the NCIS team learns that the missing 10 kilograms of highly toxic chemical weapons are now in the hands of Mamoun Sharif, a wanted terrorist, they will have to find a way to find the man and stop him before it's too late with the aid from Army Lt. Col. Hollis Mann and constant phone calls from Sharif himself. *Source: 1*

```
McGee: So this is the guy Ziva was drooling over.
Ziva: I wasn't drooling!
Tony: Please, I saw you undressing him with your bedroom eyes.
Ziva: At least I'm not the one asking him if he waxed his eyebrows!
Tony: It's important to appreciate the competition.

Abby: (about getting a tattoo) What'd you think?
Gibbs: I don't think I'm the one to ask about this.
Abby: But Gibbs, you know me better than anyone else and when you're gonna make
decision that's gonna effect the rest of your life you need the person around
you who knows you the best for guidence.Please?
Gibbs: Where do you want to put the tattoo?
Abby: Okay, you're right.You're not the one to ask.
```
Source: 3

Episodes Season 4

No.	German Title	US Title	Air Date USA	Air Date GER	Directed by	Written by
4.84	Der Frosch	**Blowback**	Feb 6, 2007	Jun 3, 2007	T.Wright	C.Silber

After catching an international arms dealer, the NCIS team learns that Navy's highly classified weapons system will be sold to "La Grenouille," an important arms dealer. To stop the transaction from happening, the team sends Ducky undercover. Meanwhile, another government agency appears to be working on the same case, with different plans. *Source:* [1]

Gibbs Rule No.4: If you have a secret, the best thing is to keep it to yourself. The second-best is to tell one other person if you must. There is no third best.

Ziva: *(about Tony's girlfriend)* Will you tell me her name if I find the pirate's copy of ARES?
Tony: Pirated copy.
Ziva: That's what I said.
Tony: No, you said pirate's copy.Pirate is a person, like Captan Jack Sparrow.A pirated copy.......
Ziva: Who is Jack Sparrow?
Tony: Johnny Depp.
Ziva: He's a piarte?
Tony: No, he's an actor.
Ziva: Oh.
Tony: *(meaning their conversation)* How did we get here?
Ziva: I drove.

Ziva: I told you I couldn't program the navigator.I'm a driver!
McGee: Ziva, I've driven with you before.I'd rather be lost than dead.

Source: [3]

No.	German Title	US Title	Air Date USA	Air Date GER	Directed by	Written by
4.85	Das letzte Lebewohl	**Friends & Lovers**	Feb 13, 2007	Sep 16, 2007	D.Smith	J.C.Kelly

A man proposing to his girlfriend finds the body of a sailor. NCIS works with local officers believing that the man died of an unintentional drug overdose. However, Abby discovers a message written in blood on a laminated card found at the crime scene. Meanwhile, Jimmy continues his relationship with Agent Michelle Lee. *Source:* [1]

Palmer: Not to mention a great source of protein.
Ducky: Ah, as I was saying, they should prove helpful in determining the time of death unless, of course, my assistant decides to eat them first.

Tony: I really need to write a book.
Gibbs: You should read one first...

Ziva: This is going to be like looking for a needle in a needlestack.
Tony: Needle in a haystack.
Ziva: I like my description better.

Ducky: However women normally hide poison in food not drinks.
Gibbs: That would explain why my last ex wife spent so much time in the kitchen.

McGee: Well, Gibbs is more interested in this. Find anything yet?
Abby: When, McGee? If you haven't noticed, I'm the only one here......Which may be the reason I started talking to my machines in the first place.
McGee: Well, Abbs, I gotta tell him something.
Abby: Tell him you love him, McGee.It works for me.

Source: [3]

Episodes Season 4

No.	German Title	US Title	Air Date USA	Air Date GER	Directed by	Written by
4.86	Wettlauf mit dem Tod	**Dead Man Walking**	Feb 20, 2007	Sep 23, 2007	C.Bucksey	N.Scovell

A Navy Lieutenant arrives at NCIS with radiation poisoning requesting that the team investigate his murder. The Navy Lieutenant is an inspector for the International Atomic Energy Agency, so the team tries to figure out who would want to make sure he didn't make it to the next inspection. However, only his two closest colleagues knew where the next inspection was to take place. Meanwhile, Ziva sympathizes with the Lieutenant, in whom she sees a reflection of her own most strongly held beliefs and develops feelings for him. It is revealed in the next episode that the Lieutenant had passed away. *Source:* [1]

```
Ziva: This is killing me. I feel like I know him.
Tony: Mossad?
Ziva: Maybe.
Tony: Internet dateing?
Ziva: I will kill you eighteen different ways with this paperclip.

Tony: If clothes make the man, what does that make McGee?
Ziva: Male Nurse?
Tony: No. Aqua Smurf.
```
Source: [3]

No.	German Title	US Title	Air Date USA	Air Date GER	Directed by	Written by
4.87	Skelette	**Skeletons**	Feb 27, 2007	Sep 30, 2007	C.Bucksey	N.Scovell

An explosion at a military cemetery mausoleum turns up a skeleton. As they investigate, Ducky discovers that they have turned up the skeleton of more than one body. The team talks to the families to try to find some link between the victims. Meanwhile, Abby is having personal problems. *Source:* [1]

```
Ziva: Last one to the party.
Tony: It's not really a party till the bomb squad says it is.
```
Source: [3]

No.	German Title	US Title	Air Date USA	Air Date GER	Directed by	Written by
4.88	Der verlorene Sohn	**Iceman**	Mar 30, 2007	Oct 7, 2007	T.Wright	S.Brennan

When the man on Ducky's table turns out to still be alive the unit must track the young Marine's actions prior to his arrival in the morgue. They discover that the marine had been on leave and used his time off for a secret trip to Baghdad. The case takes a turn when Mike Franks - Gibbs' old boss shows up revealing that the young marine is in fact his son. *Source:* [1]

```
Tony: Ever tell your dad what you were up to Probie?
McGee: Everyday!
Tony: ... wrong person to ask.
```
Source: [3]

No.	German Title	US Title	Air Date USA	Air Date GER	Directed by	Written by
4.89	Hinterhalt	**Grace Period**	Apr 3, 2007	Oct 14, 2007	J.Wlthmore Jr.	J.C.Kelly

An NCIS team, led by Paula Cassidy, discovers a tip about terrorist activity but it turns out to be a trap, resulting in the death of two agents and Cassidy, grief-stricken begins blaming herself for what happened. Gibbs and his team are sent to investigate the deaths with Cassidy joining them during the investigation. While Ducky is sure that the man who Cassidy received the tip from was dead at least one day before the explosion, Cassidy insists otherwise. At the end, Paula Cassidy dies in an explosion, much to Tony's sadness. *Source:* [1]

Episodes Season 4

No.	German Title	US Title	Air Date USA	Air Date GER	Directed by	Written by
4.90	Das Buch zum Mord	**Cover Story**	Apr 10, 2007	Oct 21, 2007	D.Smith	D.North

During the murder investigation of a Petty Officer, McGee is unsettled when elements of the crime scene resemble the descriptions in his new novel, which is half-finished. The only person who had access to McGee's book, other than McGee himself, is his publisher. The killer promises two more kills and when the second body is found, McGee is pressured to determine who the killer plans to kill next. *Source: [1]*

```
Gibbs: Nice of you to join us, DiNozzo.
Tony: I thought I was gaining ground.He has a very unorthadox running style.But
it's effective.
Gibbs: Not effective enough.

Abby: I will not reveal my sorcess even if you torture me.
Tony: Ducky?
Abby: Yes!
```
Source: [3]

No.	German Title	US Title	Air Date USA	Air Date GER	Directed by	Written by
4.91	Zum Greifen nah	**Brothers in Arms**	Apr 24, 2007	Oct 28, 2007	M.Mitchell	S.D.Binder

Director Shepard meets an informant named Troy Webster who has information on international arms dealer La Grenouille but Webster is killed. Shepard later becomes convinced that La Grenouille ordered the kill but the team are all doubting her judgement, believing she might be on a personal revenge trip which is further increased when she manages to lead the team into a trap, leaving them with no clues to La Grenouille's whereabouts after days of investigations. *Source: [1]*

```
Gibbs: Director of NCIS.
Jenny: Yes?
Gibbs: That's a job I wouldn't want.
Jenny: Don't worry, no one's offering.
Gibbs: You know why?
Jenny: You mean besides your impatience, total lack of respect to authority,
and the fact that you still haven't learned how to play nice with others?
Gibbs Yeah, besides all that.
```
Source: [3]

No.	German Title	US Title	Air Date USA	Air Date GER	Directed by	Written by
4.92	Der blinde Fotograf	**In The Dark**	May 1, 2007	Nov 4, 2007	T.Wright	S.D.Binder

The assistant of a blind photographer notices a dead Petty Officer in one of the photographs and calls NCIS. Gibbs and his team respond to the case and use the photographer's help to re-construct the crime scene through his heightened senses of hearing and scent to find out who killed the victim. Meanwhile, both Gibbs and Tony are having love troubles. *Source: [1]*

```
Tony: It's complicated.
Ziva: Complicated. Complicated. Complicated. You know, in America I have
noticed they use that word as a code for, "If I explain it, uh, you would not
agree with me. Therefore, I will use the word complicated and hopefully you
will stop asking."
Tony: Yeah, that's pretty much it in a nutshell. I'm gonna go see what Abby
wants.

McGee: Cant imagine what I'd do if I lost my eyesight.
Ziva: Youd adapt.
McGee: What if I didnt?
Ziva: Youd fall into a deep depression and eventually you'd die.
```
Source: [3]

Episodes Season 4

No.	German Title	US Title	Air Date USA	Air Date GER	Directed by	Written by
4.93	Das trojanische Pferd	**Trojan Horse**	May 8, 2007	Nov 11, 2007	T.O'Hara	D.Bellisario & S.Brennan

A man is found dead in a taxi headed to the NCIS headquarters but his body shows no signs of external injuries. Gibbs decides to lead the investigation into the man's death in preference to performing his duties as the Acting Director of NCIS while Jenny is in Paris attending an Interpol conference. When the team discovers that the people whose names were found on a list belonging to the dead man are all dead, Gibbs suspects that the list is a decoy used to distract them. *Source:* [1]

Gibbs: I had a wife like you, once, Cynthia. I divorced her.
Cynthia: Beat her to it, did you?

Ziva: Our cabbie did not take the most direct route from the Embassy.
Tony: This is America, Ziva, the land of opportunity. No cabbie ever takes the quickest route.

Gibbs: I thought you were supposed to solve these riddles Duck?
Ducky: Abby and I like to share.

Source: [3]

No.	German Title	US Title	Air Date USA	Air Date GER	Directed by	Written by
4.94	Der Todesengel	**Angel of Death**	May 22, 2007	Nov 18, 2007	T.O'Hara	D.Bellisario

Jenny returns from her European trip and discovers that she had an unannounced visitor at her home who she suspects is her supposedly dead father. All NCIS agents are scheduled to take a Homeland Security polygraph test, which Gibbs finds out to have been arranged by the CIA. An unarmed Tony and Jeanne are held hostage in the hospital morgue by a drug dealer, who is desperate to remove his shipment of drugs from the dead body packer. Tony eventually meets the man he's been trying to find all these months - René Benoit, also known as La Grenouille who is revealed to be Jeanne's father. *Source:* [1]

Jenny: In polite society one usually calls before a visit. Bourbon?
Gibbs: I've kicked in too many doors to be polite. Yes.
Jenny: I appreciate the restraint you showed by using the bell. I've been rather fond of that door since I was a child.

Ziva: I have a funny feeling doctor.
Ducky: It's teh tequilla, my dear.You've had three Shooters just in the time I've been here.
Ziva: *(looking at her phone)* Striaght to voicemail just like always when he's with her.
Ducky: Tony?
Ziva: What?
Ducky: *(pause)* Nothing.
Ziva: Oh, no, no, no.That was defintly something.
Ducky: Well, why do you moniter Tony?
Ziva: I don't moniter Tony.
Ducky: Yes, you do, my dear.Like a mother with a toddler.
Ziva: That's a good description.
Ducky: Or a woman with a wayward lover.

Ducky: Ziva it's friday night, Tony is with his girlfriend and you are worried about him what does that tell you?
Ziva: He is my partner and my partner said he would be here, and......and I have this not so good feeling.

Source: [3]

Season 5 (Episodes 5.95- 5.113)

The fifth season premiered on September 25, 2007 and marks the end of Donald Bellisario's involvement as show runner. It concludes the La Grenouille storyline which ended with a cliffhanger in season four's finale, "Angel of Death". The fifth season also reveals more background information about Gibbs' past before NCIS. The strike-shortened season ended with its 19th episode on May 20, 2008; the strike-caused gap is between episodes 11 and 12. The season ended with a two-part season finale called "Judgment Day". The season featured the departure of recurring characters Colonel Hollis Mann and Jeanne Benoit, as well as the death of Jenny Shepard, one of the main characters.The Writer Guild strike limited episode production and the DVD set had only five discs instead of six. From this season on, the opening sequence was shorted to an even 30 second duration instead of the normal 37-44 second duration in the previous seasons.

Source: [1]

Original Air Date USA	September 25, 2007 – May 20, 2008 on CBS
Original Air Date German Language	March 2, 2008 – October 19, 2008 on Sat 1

Episodes Season 5

No.	German Title	US Title	Air Date USA	Air Date GER	Directed by	Written by
5.95	Meine Freundin, ihr Vater und ich	**Bury Your Dead**	Sep 25, 2007	Mar 2, 2008	T.Wright	S.Brennan

Directly following the events from the previous episode, "Angel of Death", Tony is still undercover as Anthony DiNardo and meets Jeanne's father, La Grenouille, who is aware of Tony's true identity. The team are also led to the assumption that Tony is dead, as while watching the security cameras, Tony's car explodes and Ducky's analysis indicates the body could be that of Tony. Director Shepard reveals to Agent Gibbs and his team that she had given Tony an undercover mission to build a relationship with Jeanne in hopes of capturing La Grenouille after spending nearly ten years searching for him. La Grenouille approaches Director Shepard for protection after deciding to quit the arms smuggling business against the CIA's wishes. However, Shepard refuses his plea for asylum out of pure spite. The team tries to track down La Grenouille again and find his boat, but not the man himself. They believe he made his escape and leave, until the camera pans to the water to show La Grenouille's floating corpse while also revealing that he has sustained a single gunshot wound to his forehead. *Source:* [1]

Abby: Everybody else gave you up for dead, even Ziva.
Ziva: OK, so I may have acted a little hastily.
Tony: That's my letter opener.
Ziva: Excellent balance and weight. The edge is a little dull, but I've always admired it.
Tony: Where's my American Pie coffee mug?
Abby: Palmer.
Tony: Mighty Mouse stapler?
Abby: Ducky... Hey, Ducky.
(Ducky reaches over Tony's cubicle wall)
Ducky: My dear fellow, I never believed it for a moment. Welcome home.
(Ducky hands Tony the stapler)
Gibbs: It's not every day people think you're dead, DiNozzo. *Source:* [3]

Episodes Season 5

No.	German Title	US Title	Air Date USA	Air Date GER	Directed by	Written by
5.96	Familiensache	**Family**	Oct 2, 2007	Mar 16, 2008	M.Mitchell	S.D.Binder

A Petty Officer is thought to have died in a car accident until inconsistencies at the scene indicate that the Petty Officer was murdered and was not the driver of the crashed car. When the car's driver is later found, Ducky conducts the autopsy and discovers that she had been beaten to death and had given birth not long beforehand, leading the team to believe that the killer has taken her child. *Source:* [1]

McGee: Alright I think I know what happened here.
Tony: Twenty bucks says McGee's about to say something nobody can understand again!
McGee: The GPS coordinates came bundled in a proprietary packet. Since it was a beta, I thought......
Gibbs: I'm starting to think you can't help yourself, McGee.

Ziva: It was a simple question, McGee.
McGee: Yeah, one I would expect from Tony, not you.
Ziva: I'm just being curious.
McGee: About when I lost my virginity.
Ziva: No, you misunderstood. I'm not asking when you lost your virginity, but if you lost it.

Source: [3]

No.	German Title	US Title	Air Date USA	Air Date GER	Directed by	Written by
5.97	Dreieck	**Ex-File**	Oct 9, 2007	Mar 16, 2008	D.Smith	A.H.Moreno

Two women find a dead Marine Captain on an Army base, one of whom is his wife, the other is Gibbs' third ex-wife. As Special Agent Gibbs and Lt. Colonel Mann conduct a joint investigation between NCIS and the Army into the murder, a DIA agent is sent to overlook Abby's handling of the Captain's laptop, which contains highly classified information. Gibbs becomes uncomfortable when he is forced into a confrontation amongst his ex-wife, Colonel Mann, and Director Shepard. *Source:* [1]

Abby: These things hold over 145GB of music. That's over 45 000 songs, Gibbs.
Gibbs: I only listen to 5.
Abby: 5000?
Gibbs: No five.

Mann: We have a little issue.
Jenny: We?
Mann: You wanna tell her, Agent Gibbs?
Gibbs: No, not particularly.
Jenny: Is this issue going to involve lawyers?
Mann: It already did. It's his ex-wife. She's a material witness.
Jenny: And which ex would that be?
Gibbs: Stephanie.
Jenny: What number is she again? Second?
Gibbs: Third.
Jenny: Oh, right. You lived in Europe with her for a while. Frankfurt.
Gibbs: Moscow.
Jenny: Two years?
Gibbs: One.
Jenny: Well, it's hard to live in Moscow... with anyone.
Jenny: Do you think he should divorce himself from this case, Col. Mann?
Mann: No, no no...
Jenny: Nor do I, I don't see a problem if you conduct the interview. Do you have a problem with Col. Mann interviewing your ex-wife, Agent Gibbs?
Gibbs: Do I have a choice?
Jenny and Mann (Together): No.

Source: [3]

Episodes Season 5

No.	German Title	US Title	Air Date USA	Air Date GER	Directed by	Written by
5.98	Eine falsche Identität	**Identity Crisis**	Oct 16, 2007	Mar 23, 2008	T.J.Wright	J.Stern

Ducky is angered when one of his research cadavers is revealed to have been a murder victim and was mistakenly tagged as a "John Doe" and donated to science. The deceased man is identified by the team as a career felon, who was working with the FBI to track down a man suspected of supplying people with new identities. NCIS works with the FBI to capture him and find the killer. *Source:* [1]

Tony: Tell me you aren't looking for a man for Ziva.
Ziva: Not for me.
Tony: Something you want to tell me, McGoo?

Tony: Do people really like boats that much?
Gibbs: You work for the Navy, DiNozzo.

Gibbs: Check out the brunette at the table.
Tony: Good find boss! I'll tell you, my radar is totally shot. She's
smoking! ..that's not what you meant.. you were suggesting that she seems
interested in our investigation. A little too interested and I should question
her... not a problem!

Ducky: I hope your opinion of me doesn't waver after I've given this fellow a
piece of my mind.
Gibbs: Never!
Ducky: I warn you... this might get ugly!

Source: [3]

No.	German Title	US Title	Air Date USA	Air Date GER	Directed by	Written by
5.99	Der Mann auf dem Dach	**Leap of Faith**	Oct 23, 2007	Mar 30, 2008	D.Smith	G.Schenck & F.Cardea

When a Navy Lieutenant who worked at the Pentagon as an intelligence officer attempts to commit suicide by jumping off a rooftop, NCIS is called in to consult the officer. After Gibbs is able to persuade the officer to step down from the ledge, the officer is shot dead, falling to his death from the rooftop. Each member of Gibbs' team has a different theory on the murder, one of which includes the officer being a mole. *Source:* [1]

Gibbs Rule #15: Always work as a team.

Abby: I can't believe you would say that to me Gibbs? How could you think that
I would be leaving? Because I got a little mad? So what?! We're family, that's
allowed. I get three or four job offers every year. I have never considered any
of them."
Tony: Then why did you have dinner with that headhunter?
Abby: Have you ever had the Beluga Caviar at the Ritz Carlton?
Nikki: Oh God yeah...
Abby: Besides, it was nice to feel wanted.

McGee: Oh that's a long way up.
Tony: It's a long way down.

Tony: Color back, now that you're on terra firma there, Probalicious?
McGee: I would'a done it!
Tony: Only, ah, you didn't.
Ziva (talking about Tony): I think he's more afraid of heights then you are.
Tony: Please, I rock climbed!
Ziva (Laughing): Yeah, twenty feet, with a harness, to impress a girl.
Tony: Well, it worked.

Source: [3]

Episodes Season 5

No.	German Title	US Title	Air Date USA	Air Date GER	Directed by	Written by
5.100	Das Geisterschiff	**Chimera**	Oct 30, 2007	Apr 6, 2008	T.O'Hara	D.E.Fesman

Gibbs' team is sent to investigate a death aboard USNS Chimera, a top-secret naval research ship sailing in the middle of the ocean. After boarding the ship, they find it abandoned except for a dead U.S. Navy scientist, who died from viral hemorrhagic fever. However, they suspect that they are not alone. Their investigation is further complicated by the Navy's reluctance to share information regarding the research which took place on Chimera. However, they quickly discover that the Chimera is not a research ship, but is in fact transporting a salvaged Russian nuclear warhead. A mole in the crew staged a viral outbreak to get the crew to abandon ship in preparation for the Russian strike team. The team sabotages the Chimera and steals the Russian strike team's boat, taking the warhead with them. As the team leaves, Navy jets destroy the Chimera to cover up any evidence of Navy involvement. *Source:* [1]

Ziva: Don't you have any paperwork to do, Dinozzo?
Tony: What do you think I'm doing? I take the paper and make it work.

Ducky: You were right, Ziva. There is someone on board.
Ziva: Not him. There's someone alive. I can feel it.
Tony: A lion-headed dragon goat?
Ziva: Maybe.

McGee: Every room is empty.
Ziva: It's like the entire crew disappeared.
Tony: Welcome aboard the U.S. N.S. Houdini.
McGee: Could be a rat.
Ziva: Would have to be an awfully big one.
Tony: Or a ghost.
Gibbs: Are you done?
Tony: Done... searching the ship? We could always search it again.

Tony: Abby, where's the gas chromata-thinga?
Abby: It's the box looking thing, with the circular door-like thing on the front.

Ziva: How did they know that we were off the ship?
Gibbs: I don't think they did.

Tony: Oh, I get it, boss.It's a black ship.
Ziva: Black sheep.
Tony: No.They don't exist.
Ziva: Oh, I've seen black sheep.
Tony: No.I said black ship not sheep.Clearly the U.S. Navy is still intent on pulling the wool over the eyes of the American people.

Tony: You ever see Run Silent, Run Deep?
Gibbs: The run silent part sounds good.

McGee: I'm dealing with my boat-phobia. Tony's dealing with his rat-phobia, and Ziva's dealing with her ghost-phobia.
Abby: So, what's Gibbs dealing with?
Gibbs: Them.

Ducky: Where's my blood analysis, DiNozzo?
Tony: I'm working on it, Ducky.It may be the last thing I do.
Ducky: Let's hope not.

Source: [3]

Episodes Season 5

No.	German Title	US Title	Air Date USA	Air Date GER	Directed by	Written by
5.101	Alte Wunden	**Requiem**	Nov 6, 2007	Apr 13, 2008	T.Wharmby	S.Brennan

The episode begins with Tony retrieving Gibbs from the water and trying to revive him. It is revealed that Maddie, a childhood friend of Gibbs' deceased daughter Kelly, comes to him for help after being stalked which leads to the events of Gibbs' car driving into water. While unconscious Gibbs hallucinates that he is visited by his dead wife and daughter and is reassured that everything is fine. *Source:* [1]

Tony: This is ground control to Major McThom. This is ground control to Major
Thom. Is anybody out there?
McGee: What?
Tony: Oh. I was just checking. You've been staring into space for the last
hour. Even on the McGeekle scale that is cause for concern.

Source: 3

No.	German Title	US Title	Air Date USA	Air Date GER	Directed by	Written by
5.102	Mord im Taxi	**Designated Target**	Nov 13, 2007	Apr 20, 2008	C.Bucksey	R.Steiner

Gibbs and his team investigate the assassination of a Navy Admiral and meet a woman whose search for her husband, a political refugee from Africa, is related to the case. It turns out that a death squad by an African dictatorship who fear that the missing husband (who they only have a vague description of) will return to lead the opposition in the country. They discover the identity of the assassin and arrest him before he can finish the job. *Source:* [1]

Ziva: *(on the phone)* No, no, no, it's not you, it's just.....Well, you know, these
things run their course, and well, ah, you, you must accpet.....
Tony: Personal call, David?
Ziva: *(covering the phone)* Yes! Go away!
Tony: Somebody being dumped?
Ziva: Oh, how do you tell someone you no longer wish to see them?
Tony: Easy. *(grabs the phone)* Listen dirt bag, this is Ziva's husband.I have your
number now, I can find your address.If you ever try to contact her again I will
reach down your throat, grab your intestines, rip them out and drive over your
head! Lose this number or lose your life! *(hangs up, gives it to Ziva)* Your welcome.
Ziva: That was Aunt Neddi, from Tel Aviv.She was trying to stop seeing her
eighty-six year old, mah jong partner.
Tony: Why didn't you stop me?
Ziva: Too stunned.
Tony: Where do I send flowers?
Ziva: If you communicate with her again, I will kill you!

Source: 3

No.	German Title	US Title	Air Date USA	Air Date GER	Directed by	Written by
5.103	Gesucht und gefunden	**Lost & Found**	Nov 20, 2007	Apr 27 2008	M.Mitchell	D.North

While a group of boy scouts are on a visit to NCIS, Abby discovers that one of the boys was reported to have been abducted in 1998, leading the team to search for his father who is running from a murder he was accused of committing in 1998. The team launches a manhunt for the father, but are hindered by the son who warns his father in advance. *Source:* [1]

Playing Pictionary on a whiteboard, Carson draws a mansion,
Carson: A mansion.
Palmer draws a girl
Carson: OK... I got it... I got it... The Playboy Mansion!
Palmer: A... A... Playboy...it's a school, Carson...are you sure you don't know
Tony DiNozzo?

Source: 3

Episodes Season 5

No.	German Title	US Title	Air Date USA	Air Date GER	Directed by	Written by
5.104	Wie ein wilder Stier	**Corporal Punishment**	Nov 27, 2007	May 4, 2008	A.Brown	J.Stern

The NCIS team pays a heavy price when they try to track down a Marine who believes he is still in Iraq. After a violent confrontation in which DiNozzo, McGee and Ziva are injured, the team realizes the Marine is the subject of a secret experiment. Things are further complicated when a Senator's aide begins interfering with the investigation, since the Marine was due to be awarded a medal by the Senator and such an incident would be bad for his public image. The team suspects that the Marine was an unknowing subject of a secret super soldier experiment, until they discover that he had been secretly taking steroids in order to qualify for the Marines. Due to drug use, the Marine is bound to be discharged and his medal withheld. Gibbs, sympathetic for the young Marine, gives him one of his own unused medals instead. *Source:* [1]

No.	German Title	US Title	Air Date USA	Air Date GER	Directed by	Written by
5.105	Beweise	**Tribes**	Jan 15, 2008	May 11, 2008	C.Bucksey	R.Steiner

The NCIS team investigates when a Muslim Marine is found dead near a mosque that is suspected by the FBI of terrorist recruitment. Their search is delayed when Ducky refuses to autopsy the Marine in deference to the Marine's family's religious beliefs. *Source:* [1]

```
Tony: Am I the only normal one here?
Gibbs: No!
Tony: "Morning Boss!

Tony: Nobody likes a know-it-all.
McGee: Gibbs does.
```
Source: [3]

No.	German Title	US Title	Air Date USA	Air Date GER	Directed by	Written by
5.106	Auf der Lauer	**Stakeout**	Apr 8, 2008	Aug 31, 2008	T.Wharmby	F.Cardea & G.Schenck

When a high-tech naval radar goes missing but is found again, the team stakes an abandoned warehouse to catch the thief - using the radar as bait. But the plan goes wrong and the radar is stolen - and a man is murdered nearby. In the end, the team manages to connect both cases - and reveal the truth behind the reason of the theft. The true culprit was the designer of the radar, because he knew that the radar was not complete and if the Navy found out, he would lose his contract. *Source:* [1]

No.	German Title	US Title	Air Date USA	Air Date GER	Directed by	Written by
5.107	Hundeleben	**Dog Tags**	Apr 15, 2008	Sep 7, 2008	O.Scott	D.E.Fesman, A.H.Moreno

When the NCIS team investigates a fatal dog mauling of a suspected drug smuggler within the K-9, Abby risks her career in hopes of proving the victim dog's innocence to save him from being put down. The team struggles with the case, with the director threatening to end their case, when they find a new victim and finally manage to track down the drug trafficker. The trafficker was one of the K-9 trainers, who secretly replaced her drug sniffing dog with an attack dog in order to smuggle drugs. Meanwhile, Abby befriends the "killer" dog, names him "Jethro", and works to keep him from being put down as she attempts to prove the dog is not guilty. However, her landlord doesn't allow pets, so she instead forces McGee to adopt him which he grudgingly agrees to do despite the fact that the dog attacked him at the beginning of the episode. *Source:* [1]

Episodes Season 5

No.	German Title	US Title	Air Date USA	Air Date GER	Directed by	Written by
5.108	Lang lebe die Königin	**Internal Affairs**	Apr 22, 2008	Sep 14, 2008	T.Wharmby	J.Stern & R.Steiner

The dead body of La Grenouille finally surfaces and the Washington office of NCIS is investigated by the FBI, with Jenny as the prime suspect for his murder. The team assembles discreetly at Gibbs' house and investigate for themselves and confirm that he was indeed murdered. After evidence comes to light exonerating Jenny, Jeanne reappears and blames Tony for the murder, but Trent Kort (who has since, with the blessing of the CIA, taken over La Grenouille's business) arrives and claims responsibility. At the conclusion of the episode, Gibbs tells Jenny that the story she told wasn't accurate, and it is inferred that Jenny killed La Grenouille, although Gibbs does not take any action, simply stating, "Long live the queen." *Source:* [1]

McGee: Backing up three years of files: the bulk of our lives are in these cables right now flying back and forth in zeros and ones.
Tony: You do understand that I'm the ones and you're the zeros?

Tony: Gibbs gave you a mission. Everyone's counting on you. Just do what you do best.
Abby: Dance?!
Tony: Talk.

Gibbs: Questions?
McGee: Yeah, how do you get the boat out?
Gibbs: Just break the bottle.

Source: [3]

No.	German Title	US Title	Air Date USA	Air Date GER	Directed by	Written by
5.109	Grüne Zone	**In the Zone**	Apr 29, 2008	Sep 21, 2008	T.O'Hara	L.Barstyn

When a Marine Captain is killed during a mortar attack, it turns out that he was shot. Tony and Intel Analyst Nikki Jardine are sent to Baghdad to investigate, while the rest of the team assists by investigating stateside. The team uncovers that the man he contracted to provide soil testing hired a civilian contractor in Iraq to murder him when the captain discovers the soil sample was faked. While in Baghdad, Nikki tries to make up for a Marine mistake that led to the death of the man who helped her brother when he was wounded. *Source:* [1]

Ziva: *(leans in to see what he's looking at on screen and gasps)* That is quite a kiss, McGee!
McGee: *(grins)* Not bad for a wallpaper, huh?
Ziva: *(chuckles)* Well, you seem to be enjoying yourself. *(muses)* I have never seen a tongue quite so... long.
Tony: *(walks in, looking at them curiously)* McGee has a long tongue?
Ziva: No, but the cutie-pie he's kissing does.
Tony: McGee's kissing a girl?
McGee: You can't see it, Tony.
Tony: Why not?
Ziva: This is McGee's private photograph. And if he does not want you to see it here, then you have to respect his wishes... Or.... *(hits a key to bring up a very sweet picture of McGee kneeling next to the dog Jethro, who is licking him, on the squadroom plasma screen)* ...see it elsewhere.
McGee: Hey!
Tony: *(laughs)* Oh, McRomeo... You should save that stuff for the bedroom.
McGee: You're just jealous.
Tony: Jealous? I don't think so. What you're doing there could be illegal in some states.

Source: [3]

Episodes Season 5

No.	German Title	US Title	Air Date USA	Air Date GER	Directed by	Written by
5.110	Mann ohne Gesicht	**Recoil**	May 6, 2008	Sep 28, 2008	J.Whitmore Jr.	Schenck, Cardea & Fesman

Ziva is working undercover to find a murderer who killed five women and cut off their fingers after they died. She leaves with the killer, when Tony finds the fifth victim and the killer, having found out about Ziva, directs her to an abandoned warehouse. Before he can kill her, she manages to get into a fight with him and then shoot him with his own gun. The team is happy with the killer dead but some things are still unclear. A partial fingerprint from his weapon finally leads to a Marine who killed his wife copying the killer. Meanwhile Ziva has an affair with one of the men suspected to be the accomplice of the killer. *Source:* [1]

```
Gibbs: Always suspect the spouse!
Ducky: Speaking from experience, Jethro?
Abby: That's why I'm never getting married.

Ziva: Uno mas, Si'l vous plait.
Michael: You're mixing your languages.
Ziva: And my liquors.
```

Source: [3]

No.	German Title	US Title	Air Date USA	Air Date GER	Directed by	Written by
5.111	Falsche Baustelle	**About Face**	May 13, 2008	Oct 5, 2008	D.Smith	Moreno, Stern & Steiner

When investigating the death of a man at a building site, Jimmy Palmer follows a suspicious man who is snooping around, only for the man to shoot at him. Left shellshocked, Jimmy struggles to remember the man's face and thus identify him. In the end, the team finds him but the shooter tries to flee but Jimmy manages to stop him in his car. *Source:* [1]

```
Abby: One time I got my lip stuck in a vacuum cleaner display at the department
store. I lost, like, a quart of saliva before my cousin pulled the plug. I
still have nightmares about it. Can't be alone with a HEPA filter.
Palmer: How old were you?
Abby: 22. It was like Fat Tuesday or Arbor Day...

Palmer: Did we catch him? Did we learn anything about this guy?
McGee: No ... but we certainly learned something about you...
Palmer: Whatever it is ... it's not what you think!
McGee: If the shoe fits...
Palmer: Wait! Where are you going?
McGee: These boots were made for walking.
```

Source: [3]

No.	German Title	US Title	Air Date USA	Air Date GER	Directed by	Written by
5.112	Der Oshimaida-Code	**Judgment Day (1)**	May 20, 2008	Oct 12, 2008	T.J.Wright	Binder, North & Waild

Two boys discover a dead man, which is later identified as former NCIS Special Agent William Decker. Director Shepard attends his funeral in LA, with Tony and Ziva tagging along as protection. Agent Decker's death was ruled a heart attack, but an encounter at the funeral leads Jenny to suspect it was murder. Jenny sends Tony and Ziva away. The Director secretly brings in Mike Franks to help her investigate, believing the murder is related to a covert mission in Paris 9 years ago, involving herself, Decker, and Gibbs. While searching an abandoned diner, four hitmen track Shepard and Franks down and a shootout ensues inside. Jenny and Franks manage to kill all of the men, but Jenny dies from injuries she receives during the gunfight and her body is found by Tony and Ziva. *Source:* [1]

```
Tony: She died alone.
Ziva: We are all alone.
```

Source: [3]

Episodes Season 5

No.	German Title	US Title	Air Date USA	Air Date GER	Directed by	Written by
5.113	Schlimme Tage	**Judgment Day (2)**	May 20 2008	Oct 19, 2008	T.J.Wright	Binder, North & Waild

In the aftermath of Jenny's death, Assistant Director Vance searches for Franks, who escaped the diner after killing the fourth gunman. Meanwhile, Tony and Ziva try to locate the one responsible, while dealing with the fallout of failing in their assignment to protect the Director. The trail points to a former hitman called Natasha, who Jenny failed to assassinate in Paris nine years previously while on an assignment that she and Gibbs were working on together. Since Gibbs killed Natasha's lover, Natasha has returned to the U.S seeking revenge. Natasha, who never saw it coming, is killed by Franks, after Gibbs set a trap for her at Jenny's house. Gibbs burns down the house to cover up Jenny's death, making the public believe she died of smoke inhalation. In the fallout of Jenny's funeral, newly appointed Director Vance shreds a page from his personnel file in the Director's office and terminates Ziva's liaison status (sending her back to Israel), reassigns McGee to the cyber crime division, and sends Tony to the USS Ronald Reagan. Vance then gives Gibbs personnel files for his new team members. *Source: ¹*

```
Tony:  Status, McGee.
McGee: Gibbs out there. Vance out there. Natasha out there. Us here.
Tony:  What are we doing?
Ziva:  Waiting for the fireworks.

Ducky: Am I interrupting something?
McGee: Just Abby's nervous breakdown.
```

Source: ³

Season 6 (Episodes 6.114- 6.138)

The sixth season of NCIS started on September 23, 2008. The new NCIS Director Leon Vance (played by Rocky Carroll) became a regular cast character and Agent Gibbs' new team members were introduced: NCIS Agents Michelle Lee from Legal, Daniel Keating from Cybercrime, and Special Agent Brent Langer from the FBI. After the end of the second episode, McGee, Ziva and Tony had returned to the team, while Lee and Keating were transferred back to Legal and Cybercrime respectively. Langer was killed in the first episode of the season.

Source: ¹

Original Air Date USA   September 23, 2008 – May 19, 2009 on CBS

Original Air Date German Language   March 1, 2009 – November 15, 2009 on Sat1

Episodes Season 6

No.	German Title	US Title	Air Date USA	Air Date GER	Directed by	Written by
6.114	Aus den Augen …	**Last Man Standing**	Sep 23, 2008	Mar 1, 2009	T.Wharmby	S.Brennan

Gibbs is given the task of finding a mole inside his newly formed team. With the help of Agent McGee, Gibbs is able to trace phone calls between Lee and a dead Petty Officer the team had discovered earlier. After verifying Agent Lee's logs of the calls she is cleared. Daniel Keating is focused on next and he is interrogated. During Keating's interrogation, shots are fired, and Lee is found to have shot Agent Langer, who Gibbs and Vance agree to have been the mole. At the end of the episode, McGee and Ziva rejoin Gibbs in the squad room. Agent Lee is in the elevator, leaving, when she receives a text message saying, "Do they suspect?", to which she replies "NO", revealing to the audience that she is in fact the real NCIS mole. *Source:* [1]

Gibbs: Got work to do.
Tony: I'm on it boss. What am I on, McGee?

McGee: What do you see?
Tony: A short life. Yours, if I get caught.

Source: [3]

No.	German Title	US Title	Air Date USA	Air Date GER	Directed by	Written by
6.115	Agent zur See	**Agent Afloat**	Sep 30, 2008	Mar 8, 2009	T.Wright	D.Fesman & D.J.North

Now stationed on the aircraft carrier USS Seahawk(fictional), DiNozzo finds that a Navy Lieutenant's apparent suicide may be connected to a larger, deadly scheme. The deceased's wife is discovered in D.C to be the victim of a fatal beating, before the Lieutenant boarded. Yet it turns out that the Lieutenant was murdered in Cartagena, Colombia within 24 hours of his wife's death, and several days before he was scheduled to board his ship. It seems that someone else took his place, and may have the intention, it is initially believed, of exposing the ship's crew to anthrax. Gibbs and Officer Ziva David take off for Cartagena to help Tony with the investigation, and in the end DiNozzo is allowed to return to Washington D.C. despite Director Vance's apparent wishes to the contrary. *Source:* [1]

Ziva: It's freezing in here.
McGee: After four months in the sub-basement, this is cozy. It's like march of the Penguins down there.

Tony: Let me guess. You guys caught a bad case of DiNozzo-itis and had Vance send you down south.
Ziva: DiNozzo-itis, sounds venereal.
Tony: Okay, don't admit it. I know you missed me. I missed you Boss.

Source: [3]

No.	German Title	US Title	Air Date USA	Air Date GER	Directed by	Written by
6.116	Ein ehrenwerter Mann	**Capitol Offense**	Oct 7, 2008	Mar 15, 2009	D.Smith	G.Schenck & F.Cardea

The NCIS team is investigating a murder, about which Gibbs is acting strange. It turns out that the murdered Lieutenant Commander was having an affair with Senator Patrick Kiley, a former Marine officer who served with Gibbs. Sen. Kiley tells Gibbs to suspect a lobbyist of the oil companies for the murder, but a remark from the Senator's wife leads Gibbs to deduce that they are the murderers, and they are both subsequently arrested. Meanwhile Abby is making an investigation of her own, trying to find out who stole her cupcake, a gift from Ziva, for her hospitality after the former's house is fumigated with McGee eventually being revealed as the cupcake thief. *Source:* [1]

Episodes Season 6

No.	German Title	US Title	Air Date USA	Air Date GER	Directed by	Written by
6.117	Vater und Sohn	**Heartland**	Oct 14, 2008	Mar 22, 2009	T.Wharmby	J.Stern

A pair of Marines are ambushed outside a nightclub, leaving one dead and the other in critical condition. The NCIS team's investigation leads them to Stillwater, PA, the hometown of one of the Marines—and of Leroy Jethro Gibbs. The search leads them to a mining director and his family; his daughter is the ex-girlfriend of the wounded Marine. When the team finds out that the wounded Marine is actually the son of the director, investigation turns to his son-in-law who is discovered to have ordered the attack on the Marines. While in his hometown, the team is introduced to Gibbs' father (Ralph Waite), explores his past and the origins of his relationship with Shannon (his first wife).
Source: [1]

Tony: It might give us more than that. Stillwater High School.
McGee: That's supposed to mean something to us?
Tony: Stillwater High School. In all the time you two spend staring at computer screens you never once peeked in the man's file? Come on!
Abby: (giving Tony weird look) Who's file?
Tony: Stillwater is a small town in Pennsylvania. Coal country. Primarily known for the mine, but only slightly less well known as the birthplace of one Leroy Jethro Gibbs. This guy is from Gibbs home town.

McGee: I'm impressed with your Internet savvy Tony. How'd you find that?
Tony: I used Google.
McGee: Not so impressed. Gibbs probably could have done that.

McGee: Printed out directions, Boss.
Gibbs: Yeah? I know how to get there, McGee.
McGee: So...when was the last time that you went home?
Gibbs: I make it a point to go home every night.
McGee: I mean, when was the last time you went to Stillwater?
Gibbs: I just joined to Corps...Summer...76.
Ziva: What was it like when you left?
Gibbs: Ohhh...a whole lot of fanfare....fireworks....parades...might have been the Bicentennial.

Tony: So many questions. My mind is spinning with questions. I mean have you ever thought about it? He actually came somewhere, he didn't just appear you know? He didn't just start Gibbs, he was a boy and then he grew...
Ziva: I thought he was moulded from clay. Had life breathed into him by a group of mystics.
McGee: That's funny I thought he fell to earth in a capsule after his home planet exploded.
Ziva: No, he burst forth full-grown from the mind of Zeus.
McGee: Nice.
Tony: He's the avatar of Vishnu. He was sent to be the left hand of Yahweh. He was grown in a cabbage patch. I'm trying to pose a serious metaphysical question here. You wan't to be clever? I can be clever.
Gibbs (walks in): Just a matter of time, DiNozzo.

Tony: Jack, I've gotta know some things. I've got a lot of questions.
Gibbs: You can have two DiNozzo.
Tony: Where do I start?
Gibbs: You've got one left.
Tony: Well that doesn't count...okay. The rules? Did he learn him from you? Did you teach him the rules?
Jackson: Sorry son, I didn't teach him much of anything.

Source: [3]

Episodes Season 6

No.	German Title	US Title	Air Date USA	Air Date GER	Directed by	Written by
6.118	Der falsche Zeuge	**Nine Lives**	Oct 21, 2008	Mar 29, 2009	D.Smith	Burstyn, Fesman & North

Gibbs and Fornell reluctantly join forces in a murder investigation. The FBI is prosecuting a Mafia Boss. One key witness is a Marine, a man suspected to have been involved in another murder. Evidence from moldy rope used in the two murders links the crimes to the Mafia Boss. The Marine escapes from FBI protection to seek revenge, finds the Mafia Boss and shoots and kills him as Gibbs and Fornell try to stop him. Meanwhile Ziva plans for a vacation in Tel Aviv and Tony snoops around and finds a picture of a shirtless man on Ziva's desk (Ziva's partner with Mossad, although Tony does not know this), piquing his interest. *Source: 1*

Ziva: I am normal people!
Tony: You're normal people like the people from "Ordinary People" are normal people.
Tony: Why would one friend withhold information from another?
Ziva: Maybe that friend felt it was the best thing for everyone.
Tony: Best for everyone or best for herself? *(Ziva looks at him)*
McGee: Her?
Tony: Or him

Tony: I don't speak Hebrew, but I'm pretty sure you just swore. What happened? Your Men of Mossad calendar get lost in the mail?...Women of Mossad calendar get lost in the mail?

Tony: Gibbs versus Fornell. It's like Frazier-Ali or Rocky versus...everyone

Tony: What are you McDoing, McGee?
McGee: Working on Kale's phone records.
Tony: Thought you already McDid that.

Tony: See that prefix right in front of your face? That is Boynton Beach,Florida, my friend.You know what they got there? Sun, sand, old people.

Tony: I like to get to the bottom of things.It's my specialty.

McGee: You lose something there, Tony?
Tony: Just my ability to snoop around Ziva's desk without anyone noticing anything.

McGee: Think Fornell would lie to Gibbs?
Ziva: If he felt he must.
Tony: Says the woman who's being evasive to her friends about her vacation to Israel.
Ziva: I am intrigued be how intrigued you are by this Tony.
Tony: And I am curious that you are curious that I am intrigued. What's his name?
Ziva: I do not believe I said I was actually seeing anyone. Although it would be very difficult to go to Israel and not see anyone at all. It is quite populated you know.
Tony: Ah, that's cute. I don't see why you're having trouble admitting this. You know, you were in Israel for four months, plenty of time to hook up with someone.
McGee: That amount of time, Tony would've hooked up with several someones.
Tony: Hey.
Ziva: What is it you really want to know Tony?
Tony: Depends, Ziva.
Ziva: On?
Tony: On what it is you don't want me know.

Source: 3

Episodes Season 6

No.	German Title	US Title	Air Date USA	Air Date GER	Directed by	Written by
6.119	Der Traum vom Ruhm	**Murder 2.0**	Oct 28, 2008	Apr 5, 2009	A.Brown	S.D.Binder

On the week of Halloween NCIS is targeted to investigate a series of murders by a serial killer who posts videos of the crimes on the internet. The first two victims have scrolls with links to websites of videos of their murders along with cryptic pictures spliced in. After a third video is posted, a live stream from inside NCIS, a suspect is brought in but dies in Interrogation. Video of the death ends up on the web linking the crimes to a female singer. NCIS storms a garage but Gibbs realizes that it was a setup for them to kill the singer and a man who she appears to have captive at gunpoint is actually the real killer. Gibbs is given a Civil Service Award but is a no-show and Tony stands in to accept the award on his behalf. *Source:* [1]

Tony: Run for your life Probie. Run.
McGee: What are you doing?
Tony: Just trying to save your life.
McGee: What did you do?
Tony: Why is it always me? Well that's a good point, but in this case.
Ziva: McGee!
Tony: Too late.
McGee: Why is she sitting at my...
Tony: You're on your own Probie.
Ziva: McGee, get in here.
Tony: Plea temporary insanity. It's your best bet.
Ziva: What did I tell you McGee?
McGee: Uh...about what?
(Ziva gets up and drags him over to his computer screen where there are the pictures of her in a bathing suit, from Judgment Day)
McGee: Uh...
Ziva: I told you to destroy those. Twice!
McGee: I did. No I did. I...I...um...Tony! Tony must have.
Ziva: You did not erase those photos did you? Admit it and I will spare you one of your eyes.
McGee: I did not erase those photos.
Ziva: Give me your hand.
Gibbs: Better than losing your eye McGee.

Source: [3]

No.	German Title	US Title	Air Date USA	Air Date GER	Directed by	Written by
6.120	Kollateralschaden	**Collateral Damage**	Nov 11, 2008	12. Apr 12, 2009	T.O'Hara	A.H.Moreno

Gibbs and team are assigned a Probie to help investigate a bank robbery at Quantico. The security guard is shot and killed in the heist but only $27,000 was stolen and all of it was burned in the getaway vehicle. The Probie suggests looking into other similar cases and with DiNozzo's help finds a connection. It leads to the guard's son, a former convict, and his cell mate. Gibbs believe all parties will be at the guard's funeral, and with the Probie's help the team captures them both. Gibbs starts to believe that Agent Langer wasn't the mole in his unit and places Langer's old FBI ID at a bar wall dedicated to fallen officers and agents. *Source:* [1]

Gibbs Rule #13: Never, ever involve lawyers.

Ziva: You are fortunate recruits aren't allowed to carry guns.
Tony: I don't know if you noticed Ziva but she and they don't exactly want to shoot me.
Ziva: Give them time.

Source: [3]

Episodes Season 6

No.	German Title	US Title	Air Date USA	Air Date GER	Directed by	Written by
6.121	Verraten	**Cloak**	Nov 18, 2008	Apr 19, 2009	J.Withmore Jr.	J.Stern

Gibbs sends DiNozzo and Ziva to try to break into a top secret military facility, telling them that it is a test of the facility's defenses. After being caught halfway through the act, it is revealed that the facility is in fact all a hoax, and that halfway through their attempt to break in, the mole set off the fire alarm and managed to gain access to the main computer, which had its keyboard laced with a radioactive substance. After returning from the operation, the director explains to the team that one of them is the mole, and explains about the radioactive trace. He scans the hands of Tony, Ziva, Gibbs, and Ducky, and then goes to scan the hands of Abby. When he does the counter ticks, and Abby is placed into custody. Subsequently, Abby is revealed (though not to Lee) to have been in on the plan to catch the mole from the beginning. The team is monitoring Agent Lee to see if she contacts anyone, believing that the team no longer suspects her. After Lee makes a mark on a newspaper dispenser, she is brought into custody. Lee reveals that she was forced to trade secrets, because her daughter had been kidnapped. They let her go, and the episode ends with Gibbs concealed in the back of Lee's car saying "Looks like we're working together." *Source:* [1]

Gibbs: Just killing time.
Ducky: Would you like me to perform an autopsy on your watch?

Source: [3]

No.	German Title	US Title	Air Date USA	Air Date GER	Directed by	Written by
6.122	Domino	**Dagger**	Nov 25, 2008	Apr 26, 2009	D.Smith	R.Steiner & C.J.Waild

Agent Lee becomes a reluctant participant in helping the NCIS team stop a top secret defense plan from being stolen. Lee is used as bait to capture her contact, Ted Bankston, who also tells of having a family member held captive. Bankston turns out to be the mastermind in the caper and takes Lee hostage, as Gibbs corners them on a bus. Gibbs receives minor wounds in the ensuing exchange. Lee gives a signal to shoot and is shot and killed along with Bankston. Gibbs takes Lee's badge and gives it to her step sister who was found alive, as the team sorts out Lee's ultimate role in the plot. *Source:* [1]

Tony: Maybe that's the plan.
Ziva: What plan?
Tony: Exactly.

Tony: Don't worry, McScout, we got our Mossad hunting dog. Bark once for yes.

Source: [3]

No.	German Title	US Title	Air Date USA	Air Date GER	Directed by	Written by
6.123	Fight Club	**Road Kill**	Dec 2, 2008	May 3, 2009	T.J.Wright	S.Kriozere

The team investigates the death of a petty officer, who was killed in a car accident, but the agents suspect foul play. The petty officer's death was thought to be connected to a fight club. He was killed instead by a man who was blackmailed by a criminal using a female online profile to lure married men. When the man is found dead at the petty officer's home a fight club partner is the prime suspect, but it turns out that the next-door neighbor was behind the scheme and married man's murder. Tony engages in an on-line air guitar contest that Ziva finds childish, but she takes to heart Tony's words of having choices and the episode ends with Ziva playing air guitar. *Source:* [1]

Tony: Sorry Ziva, we don't talk about Fight Club.

Tony: I smell road rage.
Ziva: And I smell Big Wong.

Source: [3]

Episodes Season 6

No.	German Title	US Title	Air Date USA	Air Date GER	Directed by	Written by
6.124	Stille Nacht	**Silent Night**	Dec 16, 2008	May 10, 2009	A.Brown	S.D.Binder

The fingerprints of a presumed dead petty officer, Ned Quinn, turn up at the scene of a double homicide. Claiming innocence, Quinn explains he was in the garage working for the victims when they were murdered. While fighting with metro police who want Quinn prosecuted immediately, the team discovers evidence linking a security guard to an emptied safe at the crime scene. Having been exposed, the guard shoots McGee with a taser and unsuccessfully tries to escape. Quinn, explaining that he went "undercover" after his apartment burnt down believing his wife and daughter would be better off with the service benefits from his presumed death, is convinced by Gibbs to rejoin his family for Christmas. *Source:* [1]

No.	German Title	US Title	Air Date USA	Air Date GER	Directed by	Written by
6.125	Hinter Gittern	**Caged**	Jan 6, 2009	May 17, 2009	L.Libman	A.H.Moreno

While investigating the murder of a dead marine whose skeleton was found, McGee heads to a women's prison, hoping to retrieve a written confession from her, but all hell breaks loose when the inmates riot and take over the prison. A guard is killed during the riot and the inmates want only the murderer, not all of them to be brought to justice, holding McGee and two guards as hostages. The warden issues a deadline of before sundown during which he'll retake the prison by any means possible, forcing Gibbs and his team to race against the clock to not uncover the true identity of the murderer but to also save McGee's life. *Source:* [1]

Tony: Ziva, some men can hit a baseball at 400 feet, other build rocket ships that sail to the stars; I can spot a woman's smile at 20 yards.
Ziva: Her name is Hannah and she's asked me out to lunch twice.
Tony: You?!
Ziva: Did your rocket ship just take a nosedive?
Tony: No it just landed on a different planet.

Ziva: Get anything?
Tony: Yeah. An offer. Maybe his tech advisor on his next film. It's about a psycho sex-crazed cop.
McGee: Life and Times of Special Agent Anthony DiNozzo.

Source: [3]

No.	German Title	US Title	Air Date USA	Air Date GER	Directed by	Written by
6.126	Schatten der Vergangenheit	**Broken Bird**	Jan 13, 2009	May 24, 2009	J.Withmore Jr.	J.Stern

When investigating the death of a sailor, a female bystander attacks Ducky and he is stabbed in the hand with the same murder weapon used to committ the first crime. Gibbs and the team delve into his past to find clues and in the process, begin uncovering some disturbing secrets about his time as a doctor while serving in Afghanistan while dealing with the revelation that the woman who attacked Ducky in the beginning claims that he killed her brother. *Source:* [1]

Abby: Wanna talk knives?
Ziva: Always.

Gibbs: I need a favor.
Kort: Gibbs, I don't like you.
Gibbs: That's okay, I don't like you either.

Source: [3]

Episodes Season 6

No.	German Title	US Title	Air Date USA	Air Date GER	Directed by	Written by
6.127	Der verschwundene Ring	**Love & War**	Jan 27, 2009	May 31, 2009	T.O'Hara	D.North & S.D.Binder

The team investigates the murder of a Navy captain and uncovers possible treasonous acts he committed that may have led to his death. Meanwhile, McGee meets a new love interest named Claire online but unbeknown to him, it's actually DiNozzo. *Source: 1*

Gibbs: What do you got Abs?
Abby: 1989's Christmas nightmare for every parent.The unattainable....
Gibbs: Beary Smyles.
Abby: My dad waited in line two hours for one on Black Friday.
Gibbs: Six......Christmas Eve.

Source: 3

No.	German Title	US Title	Air Date USA	Air Date GER	Directed by	Written by
6.128	Abschreckung	**Deliverance**	Feb 10, 2009	Aug 30, 2009	D.Smith	R.Steiner & D.E.Fesman

While investigating the death of a Marine, the team finds Gibbs' Marine ID at the crime scene. It is revealed that he helped a Colombian woman 18 years ago and that her son (whose father Gibbs killed while on the mission there) tried to contact him about a major blackmailing, involving the theft of several crates of assault rifles from a Marine base. *Source: 1*

Tony: Oh, it could have been that girl I met at the concession stand while my date was in the bathroom.
Ziva: You need a secretary.
McGee: Or a therapist.
Gibbs: Or both!

Source: 3

No.	German Title	US Title	Air Date USA	Air Date GER	Directed by	Written by
6.129	Der Sündenbock	**Bounce**	Feb 17, 2009	Sep 6, 2009	A.Brown	S.D.Binder & D.North

A Marine imprisoned for embezzlement because of a case DiNozzo worked on three years ago is released and the Navy lieutenant who was a witness against him is found dead. Tony is put in charge of the team because of Gibbs' rule #38 ("Your case, your lead") and they discover that the Marine was framed for embezzlement and now someone is trying to silence those who really did it. Gibbs' fondness of DiNozzo is shown when he tells him how proud he is of his senior field agent. *Source: 1*

Gibbs Rule #38: Your case, your lead.

McGee: Who'd wanna impersonate Tony?
Ziva: Perhaps Jack Nicholson. You know, impersonation revenge?
McGee: Or it's a frame-up.
Ziva: Jeanne Benoit?
McGee: Overseas. Maybe it was Trent Kort.
Ziva: Are you detecting a trend here?
McGee: Tony does have a way with people.

Tony: The burning Bed. 1984 Farrah Fawcett.
Gibbs: Torched her husband while he was sleeping. Second wife's favorite movie.
Tony: Maybe Commander Davis's wife is going for a sequel.
McGee: *[he enters]* Hell hath no fury...
Gibbs: Like a woman scorned. Third wife's favorite quote.

Source: 3

Episodes Season 6

No.	German Title	US Title	Air Date USA	Air Date GER	Directed by	Written by
6.130	Paket von einem Toten	**South by Southwest**	Feb 24, 2009	Sep 20, 2009	T.J.Wright	F.Cardea & G.Schenck

The death of an NCIS agent leads Tony and Gibbs to the desert to track down the one woman who holds the answer. *Source:* [1]

Cop: Special Agent Gibbs. Got a woman who insists on talking to you. Claims she's with NCIS. Real weirdo, wearing a Dracula cape and a dog collar.
(chuckles slightly) Like she'd be with you.
(Gibbs looks over and sees Abby)
Gibbs: She is.
Cop: You serious?
Gibbs: Oh yeah, let her in.

Source: [3]

No.	German Title	US Title	Air Date USA	Air Date GER	Directed by	Written by
6.131	Alleingang	**Knockout**	Mar 17, 2009	Sep 27, 2009	T.Wharmby	J.Stern

Gibbs digs into Vance's past after the Director borrows Gibbs' team for an Investigation into a friend's murder. It is revealed that Tony has been in a slump with women since his break-up with Jeanne Benoit. *Source:* [1]

Ziva: You can't make an omelet without breaking some legs.
Tony: You're never making me breakfast.

Source: [3]

No.	German Title	US Title	Air Date USA	Air Date GER	Directed by	Written by
6.132	Der Fluch der Waffe	**Hide and Seek**	Mar 24, 2009	Oct 4, 2009	D.Smith	D.E.Fesman

A revolver is found in the affairs of a 12-year-old son of a lieutenant commander in the Navy. Gibbs and the team are dispatched to find out the origin of the weapon. Things get complicated when Abby finds brain matter on the weapon. *Source:* [1]

Ziva: This reminds me of the forests I used to have fun in as a child.
Tony: I find that hard to believe.
Ziva: What, that Isreal had forests?
Tony: No, that you had fun as a child.
Ziva: Oh, sure. My father used to blindfold us, take us to the middle of the forest, and then we had to find our way out by ourselves. Tony: I stand corrected.

Gibbs: How was the pawn shop?
Ziva: I hit a stone wall.
Tony: It's a brick wall.
Ziva: No, it was a stone wall. I backed up too quickly.

McGee: I can find an H-waffle double zigzag waffle; I can find a double zigzag H-waffle double zigzag, but not a zigzag double H-waffle zigzag.
Tony: I see a fish riding a unicorn.

Gibbs: Time of death?
Ducky: Taking a liver temp was out of the question.
Gibbs: Uh-huh. Too much time.
Ducky: Not enough liver. I suspect coyotes. You know, when I was a child I used to love liver. Mother would cook the liver of almost anything.
Gibbs: Duck?
Ducky: Well, that was her favorite. I preferred calves liver. You know, 'alla veneziana' with the onions.

Source: [3]

Episodes Season 6

No.	German Title	US Title	Air Date USA	Air Date GER	Directed by	Written by
6.133	Der Schatz des Piraten	**Dead Reckoning**	Mar 31, 2009	Oct 11, 2009	T.O'Hara	D.J.North

When shady CIA agent Trent Kort calls in a favor, Gibbs agrees to meet him at an abandoned warehouse. Upon Gibbs' arrival, he finds the agent with two dead men who claims the men shot each other before his arrival. Gibbs and the team must then work with Kort to put away one of NCIS's most wanted. *Source:[1]*

```
Tony: Maybe he had an appointment: doctor, dentist. Check his calendar McGee
McGee: ...No. Soon as I start going through his stuff, he's gonna walk in a
catch me. Forget it!
Ziva: I cannot believe it. I'll do it!
```
(Starts to go to Gibbs's desk, then pauses)
```
Ziva: Tony, watch the elevator. McGee the stairs. Now!
```
Source:[3]

No.	German Title	US Title	Air Date USA	Air Date GER	Directed by	Written by
6.134	Schach matt	**Toxic**	Apr 7, 2009	Oct 18, 2009	T.O'Hara	D.J.North

When a government scientist goes missing, Abby is recruited by the head of the project to carry on his work, but the team worries that she may meet the same fate as her predecessor. *Source:[1]*

```
Ziva: Tony, do you have to do that now?
Tony: It's spring. I'm spring-cleaning, so....yes!
Ziva: Spring-cleaning?
McGee: You don't have spring-cleaning in Isreal?
Ziva: We do not have spring. Israel is a desert.

Ziva: This is nice. Be able to work without Tony's incessant babbling. It's
almost as if he cannot go on for more than 30 seconds without hearing the sound
of his own voice. You know the truly amazing thing is that he fails to realize
just how irritating he is to those around him.
Gibbs: Ziva.
Ziva: Yes, Gibbs?
Gibbs: Babbling.
Ziva: Oh.
```
Source:[3]

No.	German Title	US Title	Air Date USA	Air Date GER	Directed by	Written by
6.135	Legende – Teil 1	**Legend (Part I)**	Apr 28, 2009	Oct 25, 2009	T.Wharmby	S.Brennan

The episode introduces the team of the NCIS spin-off titled NCIS: Los Angeles. Gibbs and McGee fly to Los Angeles to work with the NCIS Office of Special Projects—Los Angeles team to solve the murder of a marine and eventually discover that the killing is linked to members of a terrorist sleeper cell. *Source:[1]*

```
Tony: Long distance can be hard. Tell a friend from Tel-Aviv?
Ziva: You're jealous.
Tony: I'm not jealous.
Ziva: Yes you are.
Tony: No I'm not, and I'm not arguing, boss.
McGee: Are to!
Tony: Am not!

Callen: Is there a reason we're not meeting in a bar right now?
Gibbs: Well yeah, it's 10 o'clock in the morning.
Callen: I don't know what's worse: getting older or getting wiser.
```
Source:[3]

Episodes Season 6

No.	German Title	US Title	Air Date USA	Air Date GER	Directed by	Written by
6.136	Legende – Teil 2	**Legend (Part II)**	May 5, 2009	Nov 1, 2009	T.Wharmby	S.Brennan

With the appearance of Mossad officer Michael Rivkin, Tony finds himself being forced to question Ziva's loyalty to NCIS. Meanwhile, in Los Angeles, Special Agent Callen goes undercover to try to catch a terrorist cell while OSP psychologist Nate Getz discovers the startling truth about Gibbs and Special Agent Lara Macy's relationship. The NCIS team members soon find themselves racing against the clock to stop Rivkin as they attempt to capture a member of the terrorist cell but it's not easy as Rivkin is making things hard for them by putting all the members of the terrorist cell to sleep one by one before they can get a chance to arrest one. The episode ends with Callen being critically injured in a drive-by shooting and also Ziva being in bed with Rivkin, implying that they might have slept together. *Source:* [1]

Tony: Are we fighting?
Ziva: If we were you would be on the floor bleeding.
Tony: Okay, I accept that as a likely outcome.

Source: [3]

No.	German Title	US Title	Air Date USA	Air Date GER	Directed by	Written by
6.137	Geheimpoker	**Semper Fidelis**	May 12, 2009	Nov 8, 2009	T.Wharmby	J.Stern

After a security breach at the SECNAV's residence leads to the death of an ICE agent, Gibbs and the team are forced to work with ICE and the FBI to find his killer. Meanwhile, Tony finally comes face-to-face with Michael Rivkin and attempts to arrest him for operating on U.S soil which foreign agencies are forbidden to do and for also killing the cell handler and the ICE agent but the two get into a tough brawl which ends when Tony is forced to shoot Rivkin in self-defense when Rivkin tries to stab him with a piece of glass. *Source:* [1]

Abby: The bug stomp. Classic movie move. Sounds like a Tony.
McGee: Nah. It was a Jules.
Abby: A Jules? What is a Jules? I'm going to have a word with this Jules if we ever have the good fortune of meeting.
McGee: I'd like to be here for that.

Source: [3]

No.	German Title	US Title	Air Date USA	Air Date GER	Directed by	Written by
6.138	Heimkehr	**Aliyah**	May 19, 2009	Nov 15, 2009	D.J.North	D.Smith

With Rivkin later dying in hospital from his injuries despite Ziva's efforts to help him and Ziva's own apartment being destroyed in an explosion, Gibbs, Vance, DiNozzo and Ziva travel to Israel, having been summoned there at the request of Eli David, the enigmatic and powerful head of Mossad and also Ziva's father who is demanding answers in regards to Rivkin's death. As tensions rise, and based on information he gets from McGee and Abby who back in Washington are busy working on the laptop found in the wreckage of Ziva's home, Gibbs decides to leave Ziva in Tel Aviv where it is later shown that she has once again been recruited into Mossad and is embarking on a mission to stop a terrorist cell, taking Rivkin's place on the team. However the episode ends in a cliffhanger when it's shown that Ziva has been captured by the terrorists in Somalia that Rivkin had been investigating and the leader, Saleem Ulman is torturing her for information on NCIS. *Source:* [1]

Tony: "Ok. Stop right there. If this is about my Twitter page, I just want to clarify - I'd had a couple of cocktails and what can I say? Sometimes I get a little chatty."

Source: [3]

Season 7 (Episodes 7.139- 7.162)

The seventh season of NCIS started on September 22, 2009 with NCIS: Los Angeles premiering afterwards. At the end of season 6 Ziva had left the NCIS team in Israel, returning to work as a Mossad officer. In the closing seconds of the sixth season, Ziva was shown to have been captured and tortured for information about NCIS.

In the first episode of season 7, Ziva was rescued by Gibbs, Tony and McGee and upon her return to Washington, she eventually became an NCIS Agent after resigning from Mossad for good. Much of the season's story arc then focused on the Mexican Drug War and Colonel Merton Bell, a suspected murderer who hired the lawyer M. Allison Hart to represent him. Hart quickly became a thorn in Gibbs's side by regularly showing up and protecting possible suspects while they were being investigated, claiming that they were her clients.

The season drew to a close as Gibbs was later kidnapped by someone working for Paloma Reynosa, the daughter of the late Pedro Hernandez, a drug dealer Gibbs himself shot dead twenty years previously as Hernadez had been responsible for killing Gibbs's first wife Shannon and daughter Kelly. While being held prisoner, Paloma informed Gibbs that he would work for her or she would have everyone he ever knew and cared about die if he didn't go through with her demands.

It also ended on a cliffhanger with Paloma herself travelling to Stillwater and confronting Jackson Gibbs in his shop, leaving his fate unknown.

Source: [1]

Original Air Date USA   September 22, 2009 – May 25, 2010 on CBS

Original Air Date German Language   February 28, 2010 – October 31, 2010 on Sat 1

Episodes Season 7

No.	German Title	US Title	Air Date USA	Air Date GER	Directed by	Written by
7.139	Der Joker	**Truth or Consequences**	Sep 22, 2009	Feb 28, 2010	D.Smith	J.Stern

Several months have passed since Gibbs left Ziva in Israel, and no-one at NCIS has heard anything from her since. Concerned that something might have gone wrong, Tony, McGee and Abby track down her last known whereabouts, and discover that she was on a mission to take out terrorist Saleem Ulman in Northern Africa. Tony and McGee track him down to get answers about Ziva's disappearance, but are quickly taken prisoner by Saleem. Unfamiliar with NCIS and Tony's mission, Saleem administers a truth serum and questions Tony extensively about the inner workings of the agency, how he was able to find his base of operations and why he traveled so far in his quest. Unable to keep quiet due to the serum's effects, Tony recaps the three months at NCIS since Ziva disappeared, and reveals that NCIS is under the impression that Ziva is dead. He tells Saleem that he traveled to Northern Africa to seek vengeance on the parties responsible. Saleem then demands that Tony reveal the identities of all NCIS agents in the region, and threatens to kill a hostage if he doesn't speak. To Tony's surprise, the hostage is Ziva. However, just as Saleem is about to execute Ziva, Tony tells Saleem one last thing: Gibbs is in Northern Africa too, and Saleem is about to die. Gibbs had been lying in wait the entire time, and just then takes a sniper shot, not only killing Saleem but also the other guards watching over Ziva, Tony and McGee, allowing them to escape. After they all return to the office, everyone stands up and welcomes the team back. *Source:* [1]

```
McGee: I am not your home theater guy.
Tony: Don't be redonculous. Of course you're my home theater guy.
Tony: It's computers. It's your thing. If I had a thing I'd show it off all the time.
Gibbs: There's rules against that DiNozzo.
```
Source: [3]

No.	German Title	US Title	Air Date USA	Air Date GER	Directed by	Written by
7.140	Wie ein Vater	**Reunion**	Sep 29, 2009	Mar 7, 2010	T.Wharmby	S.Binder

The team investigates a bachelor party where all three guests are murdered and left in very mysterious circumstances. One of the victims is found hanging, another is found drowned in the toilet, the third suffered from alcohol poisoning and all three are found with their heads shaved, post mortem. After a thorough investigation the team zeros in on a suspect, a police officer that had been bullied by the three victims during high school. The way that all three victims were found corresponds with the way they had tormented the cop, right down to shaving his head. They also discover that the three victims had used their Navy connections to set up the illegal sale of a decommissioned aircraft, and that the bachelor party was actually a front for the deal to go down during. The team figures the police officer had finally taken his revenge and not only killed his tormentors, but also stole their profits from the aircraft heist. However, after the officer turns up dead, the team learns that the real culprit also attended the same high school as the original three victims, and had framed the cop so they could steal the money from the aircraft job. Meanwhile, Ziva deals with her feelings towards Tony and apologizes for ever doubting him. *Source:* [1]

```
Tony: Hey, you missed a shot there, sidekick.
McGee: I am not your sidekick, Tony.
Tony: And yet, you are.
McGee: No, I am not, because you're not the boss.
Tony: When Gibbs isn't here, I'm the boss.
Gibbs: Gibbs is here.
Tony: Hey, Boss.

Ziva: I was not sure what to say.
Tony: Well did it have to be said in the men's bathroom?
Ziva: I'm sure it had to be said.
```
Source: [3]

Episodes Season 7

No.	German Title	US Title	Air Date USA	Air Date GER	Directed by	Written by
7.141	Der Insider	**The Inside Man**	Oct 6, 2009	Mar 14, 2010	T.Wharmby	F.Cardea & G.Schenck

When political blogger Matt Burns is found dead after being pushed off a bridge while following up on a tip, NCIS takes a special interest in his murder investigation. On his blog, Burns had accused NCIS of covering up the murder of a young Naval officer, Rod Arnett, who Burns suspected of insider trading. NCIS concluded that Arnett's car accident was just that, an unfortunate car accident. However, unable to oversee jurisdiction over the Burns' murder, NCIS reopens Arnett's case. Things become even more complicated when they exhume Arnett's body only to find that his body had been stolen. The team suspects that Burns stole Arnett's body so that he could fuel the conspiracy that NCIS was covering up a murder. It's discovered that Arnett gave insider information to an unassuming sandwich shop owner that he befriended while taking the train everyday. Hoping no one would ever suspect the two of them as conspiring together they agreed to split the $2 million earning. As it turns out, the sandwich shop owner, afraid his scheme with Arnett was about to be exposed, placed the tip to Burns and met him at the bridge to kill him. In the meantime, Ziva resigns from Mossad as she wishes to become a full NCIS Special Agent, but, in order for this to happen, Gibbs needs to sign a consent form. The episode ends without revealing whether Gibbs signs the form. *Source:* [1]

```
McGee:  Is that pastrami?
Tony:   Mmmmhmmm.
McGee:  Can I have some?
Tony:   Nuhuh.
McGee:  Come on! You know I didn't have lunch!
Tony:   Want my pickle?
McGee:  I hate pickles.
Tony:   I know...
McGee:  (After Tony stuffs remainder of sandwich in his mouth.) I hope you choke on that.
```

Source: [3]

No.	German Title	US Title	Air Date USA	Air Date GER	Directed by	Written by
7.142	Damokles	**Good Cop, Bad Cop**	Oct 13, 2009	Mar 21, 2010	L.Libman	D.North & J.Stern

When the remains of AWOL marine Daniel Cryer are found off the coast of Tanzania by a fishing boat, Ziva's account of Mossad's operation to take down Saleem Ulman is called in to question. It turns out that Cryer had deserted the Marines to become a soldier of fortune, and had been part of the team that Mossad had sent after Saleem. Ziva's story that the ship they had been traveling on had gone down in a storm is proven false by the location of Cryers body, and the fact that he was shot to death confirms that something other than a storm had been responsible for the sinking of the ship. Using the location of Cryer's body as a guide, the Navy is able to salvage the ship in question and discovers that the entire crew had been shot to death. Vance presses Ziva for more details, but her team leader, Malachi Ben-Gidon, shows up at NCIS and demands that Ziva return to Mossad's control. Vance agrees on the condition that Malachi debriefs them on the rest of the mission. Malachi agrees and tells them that their cover had been blown and they were forced to kill everyone on the ship, and that Ziva had killed Cryer because he had been responsible for their discovery. However, when Ziva sets the record straight and tells them it was Malachi who had shot Cryer before asking questions, Vance sends him back to Israel. Through all of this Ziva was trying to get a permanent position on the NCIS team, and after proving her loyalty is finally accepted as an NCIS agent. *Source:* [1]

```
Abby:  No plan. Just go, find along the way, if you look for something
specific....
McGee:...then there's only 1 right answer.
```

Source: [3]

Episodes Season 7

No.	German Title	US Title	Air Date USA	Air Date GER	Directed by	Written by
7.143	Böse Streiche	**Code of Conduct**	Oct 20, 2009	Mar 28, 2010	T.O'Hara	R.Steiner & C.Waild

On Halloween night the team investigates what looks to be the unfortunate suicide of Lance Corporal James Korby who is found dead in his car. However, they soon discover that Korby was murdered as his organs were frozen with liquid nitrogen and that when he attempted to breathe, the nitrogen entered his lungs, suffocating him. However it's also discovered that Korby has scar-tissue from a previous poisoning and Gibbs suspect that the entire squad, fed up of Korby's jokes attempted to kill him. Someone got Korby to drink the nitrogen and staged his death to look it like a suicide. Tony can't shake the hunch that Sara, Korby's wife and a three-time marine widower, is involved, suspecting her of being a Black Widow. It's soon revealed that Private Singer, who belonged to Korby's unit, was having an affair with Korby's wife Sara. Sara also confesses to coming home to confront Korby right around the time of the crime but getting cold feet at the last second. Just as Tony is about to cuff Sara for Korby's murder, Gibbs realizes that Sara had nothing to do with Korby's death because there was someone else with a real motive: Rachel, Korby and Sara's teenage stepdaughter. Having been about to cash in on a pretty hefty trust fund and inheritance, Rachel knew the only way she could do it was by murdering Korby and then framing Sara for his death. -In the meantime, Ziva attempts to come to terms with her new role as an NCIS Special Agent and the Probie of the team as Tony begins referring to her as Probie, something she begs him not to do for her sanity but Tony continues to do it anyway. Later, in true Halloween style, Ziva gets her own back on Tony by pretending to bow down to him and as a gift gives him a cup of coffee but when Tony drinks it and smiles at her, it's shown that his teeth have turned blue. *Source:* [1]

```
Tony: Probies, talk louder, I can hear you in there.
Ziva: McGee has been at NCIS for six years. I have been here four. We ARE
agents, so can you PLEASE stop calling us ...
Gibbs: Problem, Probie?
```
Source: [3]

No.	German Title	US Title	Air Date USA	Air Date GER	Directed by	Written by
7.144	Das Boot	**Outlaws and In-Laws**	Nov 3, 2009	Apr 4, 2010	T.Wharmby	J.Stern

When Gibbs' boat mysteriously shows up in the San Diego harbor with two dead men in it, Vance, Gibbs and Ducky travel to San Diego knowing this investigation needs to be handled with extreme sensitivity. It turns out Gibbs dropped his boat off to Franks in Mexico but Franks is nowhere to be found. Franks shows up at Gibbs' house with his daughter in law, Leyla (Franks' deceased son's wife), and granddaughter in tow. It is revealed that the two dead men worked for a private military company that was hired by Leyla's mother, Shada, a powerful tribal leader in Iraq, to kidnap and bring back her daughter and granddaughter to Iraq. It was her way of trying to re-establish a relationship with her estranged daughter. Franks takes full responsibility for the shooting but further investigation reveals that it was Leyla who shot and killed the men when she saw them approaching Franks. In the end, the private military company, headed by Col. Merton Bell, is also held responsible for bounty hunting in Mexico, and Leyla and her mother come to terms. *Source:* [1]

```
Tony: That's --
Abby: Uh-huh!
McGee: It's no longer in --
Abby: Nuh-uh!
Ziva: This is Gibbs' boat.
Abby: This is the crime scene! It was flown here on a C130 cargo plane along
with two bodies and all the evidence, and now it is mine. It is all mine! So I
can figure out the mystery!
McGee: What mystery? Who the dead guys were?
Ziva: Or who killed them.
Tony: Or how they ended up on the boat. Abby: Sure, you guys should work on
that! While I figure out how he got it out of the basement!
```
Source: [3]

Episodes Season 7

No.	German Title	US Title	Air Date USA	Air Date GER	Directed by	Written by
7.145	Der letzte Schuss	**Endgame**	Nov 10, 2009	Apr 11, 2010	J.Whitmore, Jr.	G.Glasberg

When a doctor is found murdered, Director Vance shows up at the crime scene, claiming he's seen the type of murder before. The director confirms that the killer was a North Korean assassin, named Lee Wuan Kai (first seen in the NCIS: Los Angeles episode "Killshot"). The team finds that Kai has left her DNA on the victim's body for them. The director is completely surprised and shocked when Kai calls him at home and is sitting in his driveway. As the investigation continues, the team discovers that Kai is in town to kill a North Korean official. Meanwhile, McGee's new love interest, Amanda turns out to be working for the North Korean government and is shot by Kai before dying in McGee's arms. They discover that Kai is in D.C. to kill all the men who made her into an assassin as a child. Vance returns to his home to find Kai pointing a gun at his wife. Kai reveals that she is there because she wants Vance to kill her in order to finally end her pain. The director lowers his gun to help her, but his wife finishes the job instead. . *Source:* [1]

No.	German Title	US Title	Air Date USA	Air Date GER	Directed by	Written by
7.146	Unplugged	**Power Down**	Nov 17, 2009	Apr 18, 2010	T.J.Wright	S.Binder & D.North

Shortly after an attack on an internet service provider, the power to all of Washington DC is down. When the body of a Navy Armed Forces Entertainment worker is found at the site of the attack, NCIS is called in. However, without power, the team cannot use their modern electronics and must solve the case the old fashioned way. They finally discover that the dead USO worker was in fact an undercover National Security Agency agent, one of the two people who had universal access to every retinal scanner in the United States. They then arrest one of the security guards at the service provider, as he is the true mastermind. He kidnapped the agent to gain access to the server room and cut power to the entire city so that he could secretly steal top secret personal and military data and sell it off the black market. The team then reflects on how much richer life is without electronics, until power is restored and they dive right back into their computers except for Gibbs who is more than happy to take a break from electronics for a change. *Source:* [1]

```
McGee: Do you see this? Nine hours, 21 minutes! [shoves his watch in Ziva's face]
Ziva: Has it been that long? [takes the watch away and breaks it]
McGee: Why did you do that??
Ziva: Because it was either you or the watch!
McGee: It's just, what's taking so long, you know?
Ziva: Look, I'm sure we're not the only ones that need to be rescued. Plus,
things could be a lot worse.
McGee: Yeah, how's that?
Ziva: We could be stuck here with Tony.
Tony: [from outside the elevator] I heard that! I find it very interesting that the two of
you left together late last night!
Ziva: Just ignore him. He's like an annoying bug. Eventually he'll just go
away.
McGee: Ziva, it's been five years. Trust me, he's not going anywhere.

McGee: It's just like a tardis.
Tony: A tard what?
McGee: A tardis, the machine that Dr. Who uses to time travel with...

Tony: Sorry, the whole city's been de-duracelled.
```

Source: [3]

Episodes Season 7

No.	German Title	US Title	Air Date USA	Air Date GER	Directed by	Written by
7.147	Kinderspiel	**Child's Play**	Nov 24, 2009	Apr 25, 2010	W.Webb	R.Steiner

After the body of a Marine is discovered in a corn field, the team investigates at a military intelligence base that uses genius children to crack military codes. The team discovers that one of the children is making collages that contain codes with important military secrets in them, secrets that are being sold. A second dead body points to the woman running the organization, but when the young girl escapes from the safe house (Ducky's house) and runs home to her mother, the team must race to save her from her would-be murderer. Meanwhile, Ducky attempts to convince Gibbs and the team to spend Thanksgiving at his house, in spite of previously made plans. *Source:* [1]

Ducky *(in the corn field)*: Ah fresh corn! That gives me an idea. Why don't we have corn chowder as the first course?
Tony : Poker.
McGee : Sister.
Ziva : Neighbors.
Gibbs : Later.

Source: [3]

No.	German Title	US Title	Air Date USA	Air Date GER	Directed by	Written by
7.148	Die Ehre der Familie	**Faith**	Dec 15, 2009	May 2, 2010	A.Brown	G.Glasberg

The team works to solve the murder of a Reverend's son and they soon figure out he may be involved in a hate crime. Gibbs' father returns for Christmas and Gibbs tries to figure out why he has a sudden change in behavior right before the holidays. An old friend of Abby asks McGee for a favour - her nephew (who is living with her) wants to see his mother for Christmas, who is currently on a Marine ship in the Indian Ocean, but only McGee can make it happen. Gibbs figures out that it was the victim's brother who was the culprit, since he couldn't accept his brother's conversion to Islam. Gibbs also discovers that his father killed a man attempting to rob his store and he came to ask for advice on how to deal with killing another man. *Source:* [1]

McGee: It's freezing this morning.
Tony: Man up, chilly willy. Feel that warm blood coursing through your veins. Get in touch with your inner McGrizzly Adams.
McGee: Well I've got hand warmers.
Tony: Give me one.
McGee: No.
Ziva: I'm not cold at all.
Tony: The coldblooded David, like a lady Komodo dragon; ice queen, frigid and deadly.
Ziva: And I remembered to wear my thermal underwear.
Tony: I'll give you fifty bucks for it right now.
Ziva: It wouldn't fit. You're too big.
Tony: *[desperately]* It'll stretch. Turn 'em over.

Tony: How many languages do you speak?
Ziva: Including the language of love, ten.

Abby: Like you said, whoever did this had speed, strength, and agility.
Tony: I have many of those qualities myself.
Ziva: Ha!
Tony: Where is your spirit, probette?
Ziva: Bah humbog!
Tony: Bah-what?

Source: [3]

Episodes Season 7

No.	German Title	US Title	Air Date USA	Air Date GER	Directed by	Written by
7.149	Rocket Man	**Ignition**	Jan 5, 2010	May 9, 2010	D.Smith	J.Stern

The episode starts with two forest rangers finding a body at the site of a forest fire. The team investigates and finds out that the pilot was flying a jet-pack and crashed. An attorney who dislikes Gibbs tries to keep him from talking to her clients. Ducky discovers that the victim had been poisoned and was already dead long before he put the jetpack on, leading to the team to suspect a third party. They figure out that it was the commanding officer, who stole technology from private companies and the Navy to build his own jet-pack and killed the victim to keep him quiet. Later, Gibbs discovers that the sly attorney was sent by an old enemy. ... *Source:* [1]

```
Ziva: Slow drivers.
Tony: Bad drivers.
Ziva: What is so hard? You go as fast as possible, when something gets in your
way, you turn.
Tony: You're quoting Better Off Dead. I told you to watch that.

McGee: It has a range of at least a kilometer.
Tony: I don't speak Canadian. How far is that?
```

Source: [3]

No.	German Title	US Title	Air Date USA	Air Date GER	Directed by	Written by
7.150	Der doppelte Tony	**Flesh and Blood**	Jan 12, 2010	May 16, 2010	Arvin Brown	F.Cardea & G.Schenck

The episode starts when a Saudi prince manages to escape an assassination attempt while attending flight school in the United States. The team is tasked with the investigation as well as protecting the prince. Meanwhile, Tony's father appears, much to Tony's discomfort. His father is a business associate of the prince's father, and is trying to sort out a business deal. Later, the team discovers that the assassins weren't terrorists, but was in fact the prince's brother, who disliked his carefree lifestyle. However, the brother manages to escape the country due to his diplomatic immunity. Tony finds out that his father is actually nearly broke. However, he's unwilling to confront his father. Before he leaves, Tony's father tells Tony that despite their rocky relationship, he has always loved him. *Source:* [1]

```
Gibbs Rule #6: Never say you're sorry. It's a sign of weakness.

Tony: I have to break one of your rules, boss. Number six: never say you're
sorry. I let things get out of control in the hotel room.
Gibbs: Ah, it's covered. Rule eighteen.
Tony: Oh, yeah. It's better to seek forgiveness than ask permission. Am I
forgiven?
Gibbs: No. You've been distracted by your father.
Tony: It's that obvious?
```

Source: [3]

No.	German Title	US Title	Air Date USA	Air Date GER	Directed by	Written by
7.151	Wie im Flug	**Jet Lag**	Jan 26, 2010	May 23, 2010	T.Wharmby	C.Waild

While transporting a government witness back from Paris, Tony and Ziva's assignment quickly encounters turbulence when they learn a hit man may be on their flight home. With the help of the rest of the team on the ground, as well as a botched attempt on the witness's life, Tony and Ziva deduce that the assassin is one of the flight attendants. After successfully apprehending her, they discover that the man who hired her was in fact the witness's fiance, who would be implicated in her testimony but in the process of arresting him, Gibbs's right arm is broken, forcing him to do everything with his left hand for the time being. *Source:* [1]

Episodes Season 7

No.	German Title	US Title	Air Date USA	Air Date GER	Directed by	Written by
7.152	Kobalt 60	**Masquerade**	Feb 2, 2010	May 30, 2010	J.Whitmore, Jr.	S.Binder

The team finds themselves in a race against time when a terrorist group threatens to detonate "dirty bombs" in the D.C. area. As the team tries to track down the bombs, their investigation is hampered when Hart returns to represent one of their suspects. Despite this, they manage to discover that the entire bomb plot was an elaborate hoax set up by a private intelligence agency to scare Congress into approving a bill that would award private defense contractors billions of dollars in funding. *Source:* [1]

Tony: First the plague, now radiation poisoning. I'm starting to think someone really has it in for me.
McGee: I was there, too, near the car, you know.
Ziva: We all were.
McGee: But don't let that stop you from thinking about yourself.
Tony: This isn't about me! It's about my little DiNozzo makers! They've been nuked!
McGee: I know!
Tony: Do you?! I mean, sure, Tim, you're kids are going to be smart, [Ziva rolls her eyes and walks away] but mine have a shot at being really beautiful.

Source: [3]

No.	German Title	US Title	Air Date USA	Air Date GER	Directed by	Written by
7.153	Vollgas	**Jack-Knife**	Feb 9, 2010	Jun 6, 2010	D.Smith	J.Stern

When a Marine is found dead, Gibbs, Fornell and the team hit the open road to bust an illegal trucking operation. With Werth's help, they manage to infiltrate the operation and stop the ringleaders from stealing a pair of very valuable cars. However, further investigation reveals that the owner of one of the cars was involved in a fatal hit and run accident, and that the owner was responsible for the Marine's murder in order to keep him quiet. *Source:* [1]

Gibbs Rule #27: There are two ways to follow someone.
                1st way - they never notice you;
                2nd way - they only notice you.

Gibbs: Get Ziva and DiNozzo out of bed.
McGee: What?!
Gibbs: Wake 'em up.
McGee: Oh. Oh, right. Get them out of bed because it's the middle of the night and they're asleep.
Gibbs: [looks at McGee like he's gone mad] Yes.
McGee: Individual beds. Get them out of individual beds. I was confused. I thought we were talking --
Gibbs: Need some sleep yourself, do you, McGee?

McGee (after waking up, with Tony and Ziva staring at him): I'm awake.
Ziva: We didn't say anything.
McGee: But you did something, didn't you? What did you do? Did you try to put my hand in this water?
Tony: That's a little juvenile.
McGee: You drew something on my face, didn't you? You drew on my face.
Tony: No. I suggested stripping you naked, putting a tag in your too and dragging you down to Autopsy, so when you woke up you'd think you were dead, but Ziva thought it was in poor taste.
McGee: Well, thank you, Ziva.

Source: [3]

Episodes Season 7

No.	German Title	US Title	Air Date USA	Air Date GER	Directed by	Written by
7.154	Schwiegermuttertag	**Mother's Day**	Mar 2, 2010	Sep 5, 2010	T.Wharmby	G.Glasberg & R.Steiner

Secrets arise when Gibbs's former mother-in-law surfaces as a witness in a murder investigation. At first, the crime appears to be a simple robbery gone awry, but deeper investigation reveals that there's more to the story. The victim, a Navy captain, was involved with the same drug cartel that killed Gibbs' first wife and child. His mother-in-law eventually admits that she killed the captain in revenge for her daughter and granddaughter's death, and Gibbs' tells her he murdered their real killer as well. Despite the confession, Gibbs cannot bring himself to arrest his own mother-in-law. He convinces Allison Hart to defend her, and then on purpose makes crucial legal mistakes on arresting her (not reading her her rights, questioning her without legal counsel), so Hart in her typical hardball style convinces him swiftly to let her go. *Source:* [1]

```
Tony: All right, McNosy, what do you got?
McGee: From what I can gather, Gibbs and JoAnn Fielding are very estranged.
Ziva: The woman lost her daughter and granddaughter. Now her fiancé died in her
arms and her former son-in-law is investigating! Show some sympathy!
Tony: Maybe she's cursed! Like a Kennedy!
McGee: Minus the grassy knoll.
Ziva: I heard about that! The shooter was really in the book suppository!
Tony: Depository.
Ziva: That's what I said.
```

Source: [3]

No.	German Title	US Title	Air Date USA	Air Date GER	Directed by	Written by
7.155	Zwei Leben	**Double Identity**	Mar 9, 2010	Sep 12, 2010	M.Horowitz	F.Cardea & G.Schenck

Gibbs and the team investigate the shooting of a Marine and uncovers more to his life than anyone would have ever imagined. The Marine had been declared MIA after a reconnaissance mission in Afghanistan, somehow obtained millions of dollars, and married another woman under a false identity. The victim's commanding officer reveals that in Afghanistan, they stumbled across a money cache. The victim took the money for himself and disappeared. The team then deduces that a private investigator the commanding officer hired to find the victim was the shooter, as he intended to blackmail the victim. It is also shown that Ducky's mother has passed on, sometime in 2010. *Source:* [1]

No.	German Title	US Title	Air Date USA	Air Date GER	Directed by	Written by
7.156	Der Schatz der Calafuego	**Jurisdiction**	Mar 16, 2010	Sep 19, 2010	T.O'Hara	L.D.Zlotoff

The team and Coast Guard Investigative Service join forces when a Navy diver seeking sunken treasure is murdered. Both teams suspect a wealthy doctor who was funding the treasure hunting expedition is the culprit, but the evidence just doesn't add up. Eventually, they figure out that the diver was scamming the doctor, fooling him into withdrawing cash from his accounts to find a nonexistent treasure. The diver killed the doctor and faked his own death using the body. Both the NCIS and CGIS teams apprehend the diver and the doctor's wife, who was his accomplice. *Source:* [1]

```
Gibbs: I wanted to see how Jensen lived.
Tony: It says a lot about a man. Take your house for instance: clean, no
nonsense, stoic.
Gibbs: Stoic? My house is stoic?
Tony: Understated, then?
Gibbs: I planted some roses last weekend. Red ones. Are red roses stoic?
Tony: Well, they're prickly and thorny.
```

Source: [3]

Episodes Season 7

No.	German Title	US Title	Air Date USA	Air Date GER	Directed by	Written by
7.157	Holly Snow	**Guilty Pleasure**	Apr 6, 2010	Sep 26, 2010	J.Whitmore, Jr.	R.Steiner & C.Waild

Gibbs uses Holly Snow (previously seen in the episode: "Jet Lag") to investigate a murder in the world of call girls, causing tensions within the team. After finding the body of a murdered Navy reporter, the team finds out that he was interviewing a prostitute who used to work for Holly Snow and that there have been a string of similar murders. Holly makes a deal with Gibbs to help his investigation and they track down the prostitute, who reveals that the killer is jealous of her seeing other men. At first the team believes that the killer is one of her clients, but find out it is actually her boyfriend, who is the attorney representing her. The killer kidnaps Holly, blaming her for getting his girlfriend into a life of prostitution and seeing other men. However, he is shot dead by Gibbs before he can harm her. The episode ends with Gibbs and Holly having a simple dinner together as part of their deal. *Source:* [1]

Ziva: You know what, you two? I have actually heard of this. You two are having a seven-year *****.
Tony: Itch. And yes we are.
Ziva: You two are like a married couple.
Gibbs *(arriving)*: Ah, no they're not, they're still speaking. Let's go.

Source: [3]

No.	German Title	US Title	Air Date USA	Air Date GER	Directed by	Written by
7.158	Ein rotes Haar	**Moonlighting**	Apr 27, 2010	Oct 3, 2010	T.J.Wright	S.Binder & J.Stern

When the NCIS team finds a dead Navy petty officer and FBI informant, they call in Agent Fornell to assist with the investigation. Fornell reveals that a string of similar security leaks have been occurring, and they trace the source to a private security company. They also discover that their NCIS polygraph specialist, Susan Grady, works part time at the same company. After retrieving her, the security company's office is destroyed in an explosion and Susan reveals that she stole some polygraph data for personal use. Abby manages to deduce that the killers inadvertently killed themselves in the explosion, leading Gibbs and Fornell to the real mastermind: a federal judge they both had interviewed during the investigation. She went on a secret crusade to kill informants who would take reduced sentences in return for their testimony, and wanted to destroy the polygraph data as it might implicate her involvement. *Source:* [1]

Tony: What's this surprising bit of editorializing coming from the once and future king of dorkland?
Palmer: Hey, I now have a girlfriend.
Tony: The king is dead. Long live the king.

Palmer: It wasn't sand sand, like good sand. It was bad sand. Very bad sand. It made me break out in red welts.
Ducky: It wasn't the sand, Mr. Palmer, but the sand mite.
Palmer: The sand might what?
Ducky: The sand mite bit you.
Palmer: Sand bites?
Ducky: Well, sand mites might bite.
Palmer: I'm grammatically lost.
Ducky: But medically found. The tiny crustacean known as the mite. M-i-t-e.

Fornell: Thanks for doing it my way.
Gibbs: Yeah, don't mention it.
Fornell: I was being facetious.
Gibbs: Yeah, me too.

Source: [3]

Episodes Season 7

No.	German Title	US Title	Air Date USA	Air Date GER	Directed by	Written by
7.159	Rule Nummer Zehn	**Obsession**	May 4, 2010	Oct 10, 2010	T.Wharmby	F.Cardea & G.Schenck

DiNozzo finds himself captivated by a woman he's never met while investigating the death of her brother. The woman is the world renowned reporter Dana Hutton, who has disappeared shortly after her brother's death. At first, the team believes that the murder may be connected with the siblings' work on investigating Private Military Contractors, but begin to suspect that the KGB may be involved when they discovered Dana's brother was killed by a Ricin pellet. It soon turns out that the man who brought Dana Hutton and her brother up was a KGB asset codenamed "Yuri" who owned a bank account on which the KGB stashed $10 million for use in their US intelligence operations. DiNozzo manages to contact Dana and gain her trust, and she helps the team recover Yuri's KGB documents and money, but reveals she had been injected with ricin as well. With the documents, the team find the operative who killed the Huttons as being one of the KGB agents who didn't return to Russia after the Cold War ended and who wanted to get her hands on the money that Yuri had stashed away. *Source:* [1]

```
Gibbs Rule #10: Never get personally involved in a case.
Gibbs Rule #39: There is no such thing as coincidence.

Gibbs: You okay?
Tony: Not really. I broke rule number ten. Again. Never get personally involved
in a case.
Gibbs: Yeah. That's the rule I've always had the most trouble with.
```
Source: [3]

No.	German Title	US Title	Air Date USA	Air Date GER	Directed by	Written by
7.160	Kalte Spuren	**Borderland (1)**	May 11, 2010	Oct 17, 2010	T.O' Hara	S.Binder

After finding a dead Marine with his feet cut off, as well as a truck full of dismembered feet, the team begins to believe that a serial killer is loose. Meanwhile, Abby is invited to provide a forensic science lecture in Mexico by Alejandro Rivera, and McGee goes along as an escort. While there, Abby is tasked to solve a cold case involving the murder of a drug dealer 20 years ago, and Abby eventually finds out the drug dealer was the one murdered by Gibbs. Back in the United States, the team deduces that the Marine was the killer, acting as a hit man to kill rival drug dealers and kept their feet as proof. One of the drug dealers is apprehended and she admits that she killed him in self defense. Finally, Abby confronts Gibbs about the murder, which Gibbs admits to. They both agree that somebody is trying to dig up Gibbs' past, but Abby is conflicted on whether to drop the case or pursue it and asks Gibbs whether he will love her regardless of what she does. *Source:* [1]

```
Gibbs Rule #40: If it seems like someone's out to get you, they are.

Tony: I bet Abby could last longer than ten seconds playing random chat.
Ziva: You are obsessed.
Tony: You wouldn't understand.
Ziva: Why is that?
Tony: Because, being irritating is second nature to you. Me, I'm charming.

Tony: I've already earned my pay today.
Ziva: Really? What did you find?
Tony: Haha! No way. I tell you. You tell Gibbs, I got nothing.
Ziva: Look I'm not going to steal your discovery. Okay? I've have my own.
Tony: Really? What do you got?
Ziva: No way! If I tell you, you tell Gibbs.
Gibbs: Gibbs is going to find out anyway. Come on, let's see it.
```
Source: [3]

Episodes Season 7

No.	German Title	US Title	Air Date USA	Air Date GER	Directed by	Written by
7.161	Ein guter Patriot	**Patriot Down (2)**	May 18, 2010	Oct 24,. 2010	D.Smith	G.Glasberg

The team is shocked when they discover that a charred corpse found on the beach that is revealed to be that of Special Agent Lara Macy, a fellow NCIS agent and a close friend of Gibbs. They discover that the last case Macy worked on before her tragic death was a case regarding the rape of a Navy sailor. While they manage to find the rapist, the case is completely unrelated to the murder. Meanwhile, Abby confronts Gibbs about the murder he committed in Mexico, asking him what to do, and Gibbs simply tells her to do her job and file the full report. Gibbs soon becomes convinced that Colonel Bell is responsible and leaves for Mexico. When he finally arrives, he finds Mike Franks' house has been burned to the ground as well as the bodies of several of Bell's men. Gibbs is then captured by one of Bell's henchmen, who reveals that the body that Gibbs thought was Franks is in fact Colonel Bell. Gibbs is then knocked unconscious before he can ask the henchman who he's really working for. *Source: [1]*

No.	German Title	US Title	Air Date USA	Air Date GER	Directed by	Written by
7.162	**Rule 51**	Rule Fifty-One (3)	May 25, 2010	Oct 31, 2010	D.Smith	J.Stern

Gibbs's captor is Paloma Reynosa, the leader of the Reynosa drug Cartel. Her reason for having Gibbs brought to Mexico is clear: she wants revenge against him for robbing her of her father and threatens to kill everyone Gibbs has ever met, starting with Mike Franks and ending with his father if he does not start working on her behalf. When Alejandro arrives, Gibbs figures out that the two are siblings and also the children of the drug dealer, Pedro Hernadez, whom Gibbs gunned down nearly twenty years previously in revenge for Hernandez ordering the deaths of Gibbs's first wife, Shannon and young daughter, Kelly. Alejandro reopened the case of his father's murder in an attempt to keep Gibbs out of his sister's reach whilst still delivering justice, but things are complicated by the loss of Abby's report from "Patriot Down" - which has been intercepted by Allison Hart to prevent it from reaching Mexico. Meanwhile, Ziva has passed her citizenship test and is expecting Tony and Gibbs to attend her citizenship ceremony. Tony is forced to break his promise to her when the situation escalates, and he is tasked with shadowing Rivera, meeting Mike Franks during the assignment. The episode ends with Paloma traveling to Pennsylvania and entering the store owned by Jackson Gibbs, ending the episode in a cliffhanger and leaving his fate unknown.

It is revealed that Gibbs started writing down all his rules after a suggestion by his late wife and in this episode creates a new rule, the eponymous rule 51: "Sometimes—you're wrong". Tony also mentions that all rules "in the 40s" are for emergencies only. *Source: [1]*

```
Gibbs Rule #13: Never, ever involve lawyers.

Gibbs Rule #44: First things first, hide the women and children.

Gibbs Rule #45: Clean up your messes.

Gibbs Rule #51: Sometimes - you're wrong.
```
Source: 3

Season 8 (Episodes 8.163- 8.186)

The eighth season of NCIS premiered on September 21, 2010 in the same time slot as the previous season and the second season of NCIS: Los Angeles premiered afterwards. The season story arc involved Ziva's largely unseen boyfriend, Ray, and the CIA continuing to meddle in NCIS's day-to-day workings. Notable events included the terrorism and internal affairs threat during the Enemies two-parter, and the arrival of another Major Case Response Team from Rota, Spain, the team that Tony was offered to be lead of in the beginning of season 4. The season ended on a five part story arc involving the Port-to-Port killer that menaced both teams. *Source:* [1]

Original Air Date USA   September 21, 2010 – May 17, 2011 on CBS

Original Air Date German Language   February 13, 2011 – November 8, 2011 on Sat 1

Episodes Season 8

No.	German Title	US Title	Air Date USA	Air Date GER	Directed by	Written by
8.163	Die tapferste Stunde	**Spider and the Fly (4)**	Sep 21, 2010	Feb 13, 2011	G.Glasberg	D.Smith

Following Jackson Gibbs' (guest star Ralph Waite) confrontation with Paloma Reynosa (guest star Jacqueline Obradors), he is put in NCIS protective custody at his son's house. A few months later, the death of a helicopter pilot leads the team back to the Reynosa Cartel's vendetta with Gibbs, leading team members to become targets. Paloma Reynosa, head of the cartel, plays a game of cat and mouse with NCIS as she makes a wide trail through the US, expanding her cartel's influence. Tensions erupt when Alejandro Rivera (guest star Marco Sanchez), calls Abby on her bluff over the sending of the report on the Pedro Hernandez murder and threatens her in front of Gibbs. Knowing of his involvement in the Reynosa Cartel, NCIS leads Rivera into a trap at a safehouse by tricking him into thinking his sister is dead and those responsible are in protective custody. Rivera takes the bait and intends to exact revenge, but ends up fatally shooting his own sister. Meanwhile, Leon Vance, whilst putting the report implicating Gibbs in a place no one will find it, receives a mysterious text message from Eli David, Director of Mossad claiming "I found him".. *Source:* [1]

```
Ziva:  "Hello, Tony. I am back."
Tony:  "Well, hello little Miss Sunshine State. Don't you look balmy.
Ziva:  "I do not know what balmy is and I doubt it can be good."
Tony:  "Any tan lines."
Ziva:  "I assure you I don't have any. I was working. A local informant said a
Mexican drug shipment came in by boat. A deal closed by the Reynosa family.
Rivera even paid a political visit to the mayor."

Ziva:  "I thought that was the Irish."
McGee: "Doesn't go well with eggs or bacon. Why you so tan?"
Ziva:  "Why you so white?"
McGee: "I've always been like this."
Ziva:  "Becomes you."
McGee: "You're lying."
Ziva:  "Through my teeth."
```
Source: [3]

Episodes Season 8

No.	German Title	US Title	Air Date USA	Air Date GER	Directed by	Written by
8.164	Der alte Fuchs	**Worst Nightmare**	Sep 28, 2010	Feb 15, 2011	T.Wharmby	S.Binder

A teenage girl is kidnapped from her middle school on the Quantico marine base, prompting NCIS to investigate. Nicholas Mason, the missing girl's grandfather, complicates matters when he arranges a ransom drop without informing NCIS. The team find a trail of dead bodies leading back to Mason, who admits he was a part of a black operations team that worked within the law, but outside the chain of command. Someone is using Mason's granddaughter to lure him out of retirement and lead them to the other team members. The kidnapper is the girl's high school English teacher, who was formerly a member of Mason's team and is seeking redemption for his past actions by killing off his team-mates. Meanwhile, three interns are assigned to NCIS; Abby is suspicious after her last assistant's attempt to kill her, Palmer feels ineffective after Ducky bonds with his intern, and McGee must contend with an intern who shows no interest in field work at all. Using an elaborate ploy, the team manages to trick the kidnapper into revealing where he was hiding the girl and arrest him. Meanwhile, the disobedient intern begins showing an interest in law enforcement and McGee later hands him an NCIS application form. *Source:* [1]

```
Tony: "What's goin' on here. We being replaced by younger models?"
Ziva: "I am a younger model."
Tony: "If that was intended to hurt me you've succeeded."
Ziva: "And we are not being replaced. They are from Waverly University."
Tony: "Oh yeah. That's right. Director Vance's internship program. It's not a
good idea. Feeds McGee's need to have groupies."
```

Source: [3]

No.	German Title	US Title	Air Date USA	Air Date GER	Directed by	Written by
8.165	Rache ist bitter	**Short Fuse**	Oct 5, 2010	Feb 22, 2011	L.Libman	F.Cardea & G.Schenck

NCIS responds to an emergency phone call after Heather Dempsey, a Marine bomb technician, shoots and kills an intruder in her home. Dempsey initially evades the investigation, but the team quickly find evidence she was not alone at the time. Her lover is revealed to be a senior FBI agent; the intruder a hit man. They learn that Dempsey's brother was shot and paralyzed by a man named Abbott in a gang war, and that the FBI lover recommended protective custody for him after he testified to escape jail time. Dempsey started a relationship with the agent to learn Abbott's new identity and location. When he learned that Dempsey was searching for him, Abbott hired the hitman to kill her before she could kill him. Because hiring the hitman was not part of his immunity deal, Abbott is arrested. Meanwhile, Tony is excited to be chosen as the face of NCIS' new recruitment campaign, but Director Vance decides Gibbs promotes the qualities NCIS is looking for more than Tony does. *Source:* [1]

No.	German Title	US Title	Air Date USA	Air Date GER	Directed by	Written by
8.166	Schmutzige Millionen	**Royals and Loyals**	Oct 12,2010	Mar 1, 2011	A.Brown	R.Steiner

The team is involved in an international incident as they investigate the murder of an American petty officer whose case is connected with a Royal Navy ship. Complications ensue when someone tries to get the ship to depart before NCIS can properly investigate. They discover that the murder was over a large amount of stolen CIA money, used to pay off warlords and dictators in Afghanistan. At first, the team suspects that the Royal Navy liaison officer is responsible, but quickly find out that he is actually an MI6 agent who was framed for the theft. With his help, they track down the real culprit, the corrupt CIA handler who was in charge of the money. *Source:* [1]

Episodes Season 8

No.	German Title	US Title	Air Date USA	Air Date GER	Directed by	Written by
8.167	Feld der Alpträume	**Dead Air**	Oct 19, 2010	Mar 7, 2011	T.O'Hara	C.Waild

The team investigates the death of a radio DJ and a Naval Officer who were both killed live on air, and their job becomes more difficult by the discovery of various suspects. While searching for the murderer, they inadvertently uncover a large domestic terrorist group composed mostly of wealthy homeowners living in a gated community. The terrorist group feel that America should be spending more money defending itself rather than on foreign wars, and attempted to recruit the DJ to their cause. When the DJ refused, they had him killed to silence him. The NCIS team raids the community and arrests all of the members, only to find that the group have planted a bomb at a local softball game attended by numerous high profile politicians. The NCIS team are able to evacuate the crowd from the game before the bomb explodes. *Source:* [1]

Ziva: *(noticing that the barbecue is a bomb)* Tony!!!!
Tony: No!!!!!
Tony: This is nice. I missed the old Ziva.
Ziva: I can tell.
Tony: Don't flatter yourself, that's just my knee.
Ziva: *(picks up the baseball gloves and baseball)* Hey Gibbs, have a catch?
McGee: Whoa, look at this. You do know a little something about baseball, huh?
Ziva: Yeah, my father taught me.

Source: [3]

No.	German Title	US Title	Air Date USA	Air Date GER	Directed by	Written by
8.168	Genie und Wahnsinn	**Cracked**	Oct 26, 2010	Mar 15, 2011	T.Wharmby	N.Mirante-Matthews

The NCIS team investigate the death of a Navy researcher who was hit by a bus in the middle of a busy street. They are surprised to find that her entire body is covered in elaborate mathematical formulae, but begin to suspect her death was nothing more than an accident after finding evidence that she was becoming increasingly paranoid. Recognizing the researcher as a kindred spirit because they share similar thought processes, Abby becomes fixated on solving her equations and vows to finish to the work that the victim originally started. Unfortunately her new-found obsession soon begins driving a wedge between her and the rest of the team but thanks to Gibbs and the victim's mother, Abby eventually regains her priorities and resumes working on the case. As the team discover that the researcher was being poisoned, Abby deduces that the formula is a method of converting bacteria into fuel. The trail leads back to a jealous co-worker, who poisoned the researcher in order to take her job.
Meanwhile, Tony's latest fling causes trouble when she suggests role playing, but refuses to tell Tony what she has in mind. Her fantasy is later revealed to be Tony Manero from Saturday Night Fever, evidenced by a very uncomfortable Tony attempting to sneak out of the Navy yard in a white disco suit. *Source:* [1]

Abby: "McGee. You're here. I've had some breakthroughs. Or, maybe it's more like some little bursts of inspiration because if I had a breakthrough I would have all the answers but I don't. Not yet, but I'm close. I know I am cuz I can feel it. I have a tingling feeling going up and down my spine..."
McGee: "How many Caf Pows you had today?"
Abby: "Um, eleven... teen"
McGee: "Did you even go home last night?"
Abby: "I've been inputting the raw data from the writings trying to crack the code to the formula and then BAM it hit me
McGee: "Then you think we should find him."
Abby: "Lt Thorson, she had a whole life out there somewhere. She was on a journey and it's my duty to follow it. That's how we're gonna find out who killed her. I can't do it alone, McGee. I need you to come with me."

Source: [3]

Episodes Season 8

No.	German Title	US Title	Air Date USA	Air Date GER	Directed by	Written by
8.169	Mark 15	**Broken Arrow**	Nov 9, 2010	Mar 22, 2011	A.Brown	F.Cardea & G.Schenck

When investigating a murder of a former Navy Commander and friend of Vice Admiral Chase, the team stumbles across a piece of an old nuclear bomb that had been lost during the Cold War. Because the victim had connections to Tony's father, they track him down and question him. Eventually, much to Tony's annoyance, Gibbs recruits DiNozzo Sr. to use his contacts to infiltrate a private party attended by arms dealers. They discover that the CEO of a salvage company stumbled across the nuclear bomb and plans to sell it on the black market. The CEO is arrested, and both DiNozzos finally reconcile their differences with one another. *Source:* [1]

McGee: "Mmm... Mmmm... Nutter Butter."
Tony: "This is surreal. I feel like I'm in a James Bond movie directed by Fulani. I'm on a stakeout watching my father and Ziva go undercover while you munch on a Nutter Butter."
Ziva: "We are approaching the house."
McGee: "Alright, Ziva. We read you loud and clear."
DiNozzo Sr.: "You look ravishing, Sophia." (DiNozzo Sr. puts his hand on her back.)
McGee: "Oh... oh... there it is."
Ziva: "Uh, uh."
Tony: "This is the beginning of the end of my career."
McGee: (in the house.) "Getting a solid image off the spy cam broach."
DiNozzo Sr.: "There's Dan Mayfield. Come on. I'll introduce you to him."

Gibbs: "Come on DiNozzo, give me something."
Tony: "Uh. No luck on the money trail, Boss."
Gibbs: "McGee."
McGee: "Found several IMs in Thorson's email cash. One's a video. It's a man telling her she's an ungrateful ***** and if she leaves him, he will make her life hell.
Tony: "Wow. Mel Gibson much?"
Ziva: "Huh. There was no evidence Lt Thorson had a boyfriend."
Gibbs: "McGee."
McGee: "Yep. Running the IP address. Ok, ah, this is not her boyfriend. It's her boss." *Source:* [3]

No.	German Title	US Title	Air Date USA	Air Date GER	Directed by	Written by
8.170	Fremde Feinde	**Enemies Foreign**	Nov 16, 2010	Mar 29, 2011	D.Smith	J.Stern

Vance beruft eine Revisionskonferenz ein. Die Teilnehmer sind ehemalige Direktoren und hochrangige Agenten. Auch ein alter Bekannter kündigt seinen Besuch an: Eli David. Er war vor vielen Jahren bei Vance' erstem Ontrag dabei. Plötzlich tauchen drei Palästinenser on, die Eli ans Leder wollen. Gibbs und seine Leute nehmen einen von ihnen fest, ein zweiter wird erschossen, doch der Anführer kann entkommen. Gibbs versucht, Eli und die anderen über Funk zu erreichen - ohne Erfolg. *Source:* [1]

The team is designated to protect Eli David (Mossad Director & Ziva's father) during a NCIS conference. They must deal with three Palestinian terrorists trying to kill him. The episode ends on a cliffhanger when, after an attack by the terrorists at the conference apparently fails, Vance and David go to a safe house. Gibbs cannot reach them on the radio and Officer Hadar is shown to be lying dead at the safe house. *Source:* [3]

Episodes Season 8

No.	German Title	US Title	Air Date USA	Air Date GER	Directed by	Written by
8.171	Vertraute Feinde	**Enemies Domestic**	Nov 23, 2010	Apr 5, 2011	M.Horowitz	J.Stern

Gibbs arrives at the scene to find Hadar dead, Vance critically injured, and Eli missing. Eventually, the team tracks down Eli, who had gone into hiding to elude his assassins. They then deduce that the man who planted the bomb is an insider at NCIS. During the episode, Gibbs revisits Operation Trident, Vance's first job with NIS and when he met Eli David. Gibbs originally comes to the conclusion that Eli tried to have Vance killed during the op by tipping off his primary target: a Soviet operative called the Russian. When Eli is found, it is revealed that Vance and Eli had actually worked together during the op to stop the Russian and his hit team which was the career builder for Vance. The insider in NCIS was the same person who mounted the operation in Amsterdam and whose plan was foiled by Vance and Eli. It is revealed that the insider is Riley McAllister, former head of the San Diego field office, and that he mounted the operation so that his area of expertise, Russia, would come back into a post-Cold War play which would have allowed him to become Director. He had hired the Russian, the same man that he later sent Gibbs to assassinate in Paris along with Jenny Shepard, to kill Vance and he had set up the bomb at the safe house to have revenge on Vance and Eli. He then tries to kill Vance in his hospital room... *Source:* [1]

No.	German Title	US Title	Air Date USA	Air Date GER	Directed by	Written by
8.172	Der Zeuge	**False Witness**	Dec 14, 2010	Apr 17, 2011	J.Whitmore, Jr.	S.Binder

The NCIS team investigates the disappearance of a Navy Petty Officer who is the sole witness in an upcoming murder trial. Meanwhile, Ziva and McGee attempt to discover the reason for Tony's strange behavior. Annie Wersching guest stars as Deputy District Attorney Gail Walsh. *Source:* [1]

No.	German Title	US Title	Air Date USA	Air Date GER	Directed by	Written by
8.173	Schiffe in der Nacht	**Ships in the Night**	Jan 11, 2011	Apr 26, 2011	T.Wright	R.Steiner & C.Waild

Gibbs and the NCIS team partner with Coast Guard Investigative Service (CGIS) Agent Abigail Borin to investigate the murder of a Marine First Lieutenant on a dinner cruise. The team learns of the victim's wealth, opening up new lines of investigation. The victim was the heir of a multimillion dollar corporation, and was intending to use his ownership to turn the corporation into a charity organization. Piecing together the clues, the team discovers that the victim's death was the result of a conspiracy between his sister, the family lawyer, and the corporation's CFO. Later, one of the victim's squadmates, who is also a lawyer, arrives at NCIS to deliver his last will and testament, which was intended to carry out the victim's wishes to reform his company. *Source:* [1]

No.	German Title	US Title	Air Date USA	Air Date GER	Directed by	Written by
8.174	Nichts fragen, nichts sagen	**Recruited**	Jan 18, 2011	May 3, 2011	A.Brown	G.Glasberg

A petty officer's recruitment session at a college fair comes to a fatal end, prompting the NCIS team to solve his murder. The team learns of the petty officer's homosexuality, leading Gibbs to classify the murder as a possible hate crime. Ducky's predecessor at NCIS, Dr. Magnus (Bob Newhart), pays a visit. The team tracks down several suspects, but Gibbs eventually figures out that the killer was the father of one of the students the petty officer was advising. The father did not realize the petty officer was trying to help his son deal with his homosexuality, and feared he was attempting to start a relationship with him. Meanwhile, Magnus reveals the true reason for his visit; he is suffering from Alzheimer's disease and he was hoping that coming back to NCIS would help him regain his memories. To help Magnus, Ducky gives him a collection of pictures of all of the people Magnus had helped... *Source:* [1]

Episodes Season 8

No.	German Title	US Title	Air Date USA	Air Date GER	Directed by	Written by
8.175	Die Kunst des Überlebens	**Freedom**	Feb 1, 2011	Jun 21, 2011	C.Ross, Jr.	N.Mirante-Matthews

The team investigates the murder of a marine. They find out his Marine wife (Christina Cox) was abused and that the husband had an affair. They find numerous suspects, but eventually narrow it down to a bar owner that the wife was also having an affair with. He admits to the murder because he felt the marine didn't deserve to have a wife like her. Meanwhile, McGee becomes the victim of identity theft, as somebody starts using his credit card to buy various expensive items. Tony tracks down the identity thief, who turns out to be the son of McGee's landlady. The boy remarks that he stole McGee's identity because he felt he was too boring and didn't take time to enjoy life. Also, since the purchases were clearly the result of fraud, McGee is only liable for $50. Together, Tony and the boy manage to convince McGee to come with them to buy video games. *Source:* [1]

No.	German Title	US Title	Air Date USA	Air Date GER	Directed by	Written by
8.176	Der Schlussstrich	**A Man Walks Into a Bar ...**	Feb 8, 2011	Jun 28, 2011	J.Whitmore, Jr.	G.Glasberg

A naval commander is found dead in his rack aboard ship, apparently murdered. The NCIS team investigates while having to deal with mandatory psychological evaluations conducted by Dr. Rachel Cranston, who is eventually revealed to be the older sister of their former colleague and friend, Agent Caitlin Todd. It is discovered that the commander had actually committed suicide due to facing mandatory retirement and having no other life other than the Navy, and his colleagues had disguised the suicide out of respect for him. *Source:* [1, 2]

No.	German Title	US Title	Air Date USA	Air Date GER	Directed by	Written by
8.177	Die schöne Tochter	**Defiance**	Feb 15, 2011	Jul 5, 2011	D.Smith	F.Cardea & G.Schenck

A botched assassination attempt in Belgravia forces NCIS to protect the Defense Minister's daughter Adriana, who is studying in the U.S. While the team is busy guarding Adriana, Gibbs attempts to investigate the death of the Marine who was killed protecting the minister. Meanwhile, Adriana begins developing a crush on McGee, but she is suddenly kidnapped by two armed attackers. Furious at their failure, Vance orders the team to solve the case in 48 hours or he will take McGee and Dinozzo's badges. The team discovers that Adriana, who disagreed with her father's policies, arranged her own kidnapping to pressure him. However, one of the conspirators becomes greedy and decides to hold her for ransom. Fortunately, the team is able to rescue her, but are unable to arrest her for her role in the plot due to diplomatic immunity. McGee is left to wonder if Adriana really did have feelings for him or if it was all just an act. *Source:* [1]

Episodes Season 8

No.	German Title	US Title	Air Date USA	Air Date GER	Directed by	Written by
8.178	Max Destructo	**Kill Screen**	Feb 22, 2011	Jul 12, 2011	T.Wharmby	S.Kriozere & S.D.Binder

The discovery of some extracted teeth and dismembered digits in a purse results in an NCIS investigation when they are identified as belonging to a Marine. As the team tries to track down the killer, an investigator from an electronic security firm arrives, having traced the source of a number of computer hackings to NCIS. This makes McGee nervous as he had regularly illegally hacked into government computers under Gibbs' orders. The team manages to track down Maxine, who is the dead Marine's girlfriend and is an avid gamer and computer expert. She begins to take a liking to McGee. However, McGee tries to maintain his distance due to the events in "Defiance". She reveals that she had accidentally uncovered some sort of encrypted code in an MMORPG which turns out to be a program capable of hacking the Pentagon. The team tracks down the programmer responsible and shuts down his program, but he is found dead. Gibbs and McGee deduce that the investigator that arrived earlier was behind the killings, since news of such a threat to American security could ruin his career. Later, Dinozzo manipulates events to get McGee to start dating Maxine. *Source:* [1]

No.	German Title	US Title	Air Date USA	Air Date GER	Directed by	Written by
8.179	Das Geld anderer Leute	**One Last Score**	Mar 1, 2011	Jul 26, 2011	M.Weatherly	J.Stern

NCIS discovers that one of its former investigative assistants found brutally stabbed to death was selling details for how to rob a warehouse full of valuable possessions. They discover that the warehouse contains items seized from a former Navy officer (JoBeth Williams) who used a Ponzi scheme to cheat many people out of their money. While investigating the warehouse, the team finds that something hidden in one of her desks was stolen. In order to find the killer, Gibbs makes a deal with the officer to downgrade her sentence to house arrest in return for divulging his identity. However, it is a ploy by Gibbs to lure out the real killer, a robber who lost his money trying to launder it through the officer's accounts. The officer grabs her notebook containing the accounts where she hid her money and flees, technically breaking her house arrest agreement. Gibbs and Ziva swoop in, arresting both the killer and the officer while at the same time getting the evidence they needed to put her away for life. Meanwhile, budget cuts cause personnel to be reorganized in NCIS, including the transfer of the Spain team to Washington DC. Tony immediately becomes infatuated with the new team leader, who apparently returns his feelings. *Source:* [1]

No.	German Title	US Title	Air Date USA	Air Date GER	Directed by	Written by
8.180	Das Geständnis	**Out of the Frying Pan**	Mar 22, 2011	Aug 2, 2011	T.O'Hara	Carroll, Steiner & Waild

Director Vance has Gibbs and his team assigned to the case of a drug-addicted teenager accused of patricide. Gibbs begins to question Vance's motives when the NCIS team begin to find inconsistencies in the investigation that lead him to believe his suspect is innocent. Tensions between Gibbs and Vance - fuelled by budget cuts and re-assignments in previous episodes - come to a head when Vance admits the victim was a close friend. After a lengthy investigation, NCIS discover that the boy's runaway mother had recently tried to re-enter his life, and killed his father in a rage when he refused to let the two meet. . *Source:* [1]

Episodes Season 8

No.	German Title	US Title	Air Date USA	Air Date GER	Directed by	Written by
8.181	Ein offenes Buch	**Tell-All**	Mar 29, 2011	Aug 29, 2011	K.R.Sullivan	A.Bartels

A dying message from a naval officer attached to the Defense Intelligence Agency leads Gibbs' team in search of a manuscript containing military information. As the team investigates further, they find the body of a murdered FBI agent, and discover that both victims were involved in the writing of a book exposing secret anti-terrorist operations. However, the team is forced to track down the anonymous author of the book when Navy intelligence officers destroy all copies of the book. With the author's help (who is also a former Marine Lieutenant who was discharged for a failed anti-terrorist operation), the manage to arrest an arms dealer who had stolen a shipment of military weapons, but find out that she wasn't the killer. With this new information, as well as new evidence from Abby, Gibbs deduces that the FBI agent's husband is the killer, since he mistakenly believed that his wife was having an affair. *Source:* [1]

No.	German Title	US Title	Air Date USA	Air Date GER	Directed by	Written by
8.182	Der Hafenmörder	**Two-Faced**	Apr 5, 2011	Sep 5, 2011	T.Wright	Mirante-Matthews&Steiner

The body of a seaman is found wrapped in plastic and doused with a hospital-grade cleanser, hallmarks of a serial killer known as the "Port-to-Port" killer who kills service personnel when they make landfall. Vance creates a task force to catch the killer, appointing Barrett as lead investigator as she had been tracking the killer since he struck in Rota, Spain. Tensions arise within the MCRT when Gibbs suspects Barret and DiNozzo are sleeping together, compromising the loyalties of the team. Ziva discovers her boyfriend Ray is a secret CIA liaison to NCIS and questions the entire nature of their relationship when she catches him in a lie. After several dead ends and the discovery of another victim (bringing the known total to five), the episode ends with Ziva and DiNozzo in a bar, discovering a human eyeball floating in a glass of gin and tonic sent by an unidentified patron. *Source:* [1]

No.	German Title	US Title	Air Date USA	Air Date GER	Directed by	Written by
8.183	Spiel der Masken	**Dead Reflection**	Apr 12, 2011	Oct 17, 2011	W.Webb	G.Schenck & F.Cardea

The Major Case Response Team investigates a murder in the Pentagon that was caught on camera. Complications arise when the killer himself is found dead in an apparent car accident, but Ducky claims it was impossible for him to have committed the murder that was caught on tape as he died two days earlier; eventually the team discovers the real killer was using an advanced silicone mask to impersonate the deceased so he could tamper with evidence implicating him in a botched special forces mission. Meanwhile, after trying to figure out the mystery of the eye from "Two-Faced", E.J. and Palmer discover that the eye from the previous episode can open MTAC when scanned. *Source:* [1]

Episodes Season 8

No.	German Title	US Title	Air Date USA	Air Date GER	Directed by	Written by
8.184	Besser spät als nie	**Baltimore**	May 3, 2011	Oct 24, 2011	T.O'Hara	S.Binder

After sending the NCIS team a message in the form of the eye in "Two-Faced" - revealed to belong to a person whose identity is classified - the Port to Port Killer seems to have struck with another victim: Danny Price, formerly DiNozzo's partner in the Baltimore P.D. homicide squad. Believing that the Port to Port Killer may have a connection to DiNozzo, the team begins to concentrate on his time in Baltimore. Inconsistencies in the autopsy reports lead them to suspect there is a copycat killer on the loose, and it is eventually revealed that a mistake caused by Palmer in a report sent out to law enforcement agencies gave the copycat killer the necessary knowledge to replicate the Port to Port Killer with near-perfect accuracy. Because of Palmer's mistake, NCIS is able to catch a would-be copycat before he can kill, as well as find Price's murderer - DiNozzo's former captain in Baltimore. The episode is intercut with flashbacks showing DiNozzo's first meeting with Gibbs in which DiNozzo arrested Gibbs while he was working undercover on a money laundering case. DiNozzo joins NCIS after finding himself unable to work with Price in the Baltimore PD, but unwilling to expose his former partner. *Source:* [1]

No.	German Title	US Title	Air Date USA	Air Date GER	Directed by	Written by
8.185	Schwanengesang	**Swan Song (1)**	May 10, 2011	Oct 31, 2011	T.Wharmby	J.Stern

While chasing the Port to Port Killer, NCIS is placed on high alert when evidence comes to light that he has infiltrated the Navy Yard. They learn that his latest victim survived because somebody intervened and lost an eye in the process: the team's on-again, off-again enemy, Trent Kort. Kort names the Port to Port Killer as Lt. Jonas Cobb (Kerr Smith), the first member of a CIA assassination team who cracked under inhumane training. Kort was sent to locate Cobb and eliminate him. As the NCIS team close in on Cobb, they suffer a personal tragedy when Mike Franks is killed after attempting to apprehend him. With Cobb injured, armed and unaccounted for, Gibbs confronts Leon Vance over his decisions in recent weeks. Vance admits that the decision to put E.J. Barrett in charge of the case came from higher up. Gibbs realizes that Cobb identifies with him, and is likely targeting E.J. The episode ends with E.J. ignoring Vance's orders and attempting to apprehend Cobb. However, Cobb ambushes E.J. and they both get into a struggle, which E.J. begins to slowly lose. *Source:* [1]

No.	German Title	US Title	Air Date USA	Air Date GER	Directed by	Written by
8.186	Operation Frankenstein	**Pyramid (2)**	May 17, 2011	Nov 8, 2011	D.Smith	G.Glasberg

Having learned the identity of the Port-to-Port killer after the death of Mike Franks, Gibbs and his team prepare for the worst when he makes his final strike close to the heart of NCIS, leading Ziva into a trap. When Ziva is found by McGee, DiNozzo, Gibbs and Ray Cruz, she reveals that it was misdirection while the killer, Lt. Jonas Cobb, infiltrates NCIS to target the people he holds responsible for turning him into a killer as a part of "Operation Frankenstein": Leon Vance, Trent Kort and the Secretary of the Navy. Everything he has done since killing his first victim in Spain has been with the sole intention of finding them - but knowing that the Secretary of the Navy is under twenty-four hour protection, Cobb changes tactics and instead targets E.J. Barrett who is not only the person who has been investigating him from the beginning of his killing spree, but is also the Secretary of the Navy's niece. The NCIS team are able to track Cobb back to the facility where he was put through his training and is seen "training" Trent Kort, Jimmy Palmer and Barrett. He claims he only ever did what he thought was right, but refuses to surrender and is shot and killed by Gibbs and Vance. The Secretary of the Navy resigns over the affair, Trent Kort goes into hiding in Israel and Mike Franks is given a state funeral in a coffin built by Gibbs. The episode ends with DiNozzo being given a classified assignment to "handle" an unknown person and that an NCIS agent is suspected of selling classified information. *Source:* [1]

Sources

Sources Text:

[1] Wikipedia, DL on Nov 29, 2011
via http://en.wikipedia.org/wiki/NCIS_(TV_series)

[2] NCIS Fan Site NCIS FANWIKI, DL on Nov 29, 2011
via http://www.ncisfanwiki.com/page/NCIS%3A+Gibbs+Rules

[3] NCIS Fan Site NCIS FANWIKI NCIS Quotes, DL on Nov 29, 2011
via http://www.ncisfanwiki.com/page/NCIS+Quotes

Other used Sources:

NCIS FAN private website: www.ncisfan.org/

CBS Broadcasting: www.cbs.com/shows/ncis/

Private website with forum: www.forum.navy-cis.de/

Serienjunkies.de: www.serienjunkies.de/ncis/

TV-Serieninfos: www.tvsi.de/krimiserien/navy_CIS.php

Source Poto:

Cover-/Inside-Photo by Jerry Avenaim (http://en.wikipedia.org/wiki/Jerry_Avenaim), DL on Nov 26, 2011
via http://de.wikipedia.org/w/index.php?title=Datei:Mark_Harmon_1_edit1.jpg&filetimestamp=20080805230925

The author holds no connection what so ever with Belisarius Productions, CBS Broadcasting or Paramount Pictures.